BLESS US,
O GOD

To my daughter, Gail, and grandsons,
Jason and David, who patiently listened
to my stories, and to the many individuals
and groups here at home and around the
world who touched and influenced my life.

BLESS US, O GOD

*Services and Prayers
for Special Days*

Dorothy D. France

CHALICE
PRESS

ST. LOUIS, MISSOURI

Unless otherwise indicated, all scripture quotations are from *Revised Standard Version* of the Bible, copyrighted 1946,1952, 1971, 1973 by the Division of the Christian Education of the National Council of Churches in the United States of America.

Scripture quotations marked (TEV) are taken from the *Today's English Version* © 1976 by American Bible Society. Used by Permission.

Lyrics from "Freedom Isn't Free" on page 67 are used with permission © 2007 Up With People, Inc.

"Take My Hands" on page 89 © 1967, OCP Publications, 5536 N.E. Hassalo, Portland, OR 97213. All rights reserved. Used with permission.

Excerpt on pages 103–104 is from *Extending the Table* by Joetta Handrich Schlabach. Copyright © 1991 by Herald Press, Scottdale, PA 15683. All rights reserved. Used by permission.

Cover art: © The Crosiers
Cover and interior design: Elizabeth Wright

Visit Chalice Press on the World Wide Web at
www.chalicepress.com

10 9 8 7 6 5 4 3 2 1   07 08 09 10 11 12

Library of Congress Cataloging-in-Publication Data
France, Dorothy D.
  Bless us, O God : services and prayers for special days /
Dorothy D. France.
    p. cm.
Includes bibliographical references.
    ISBN-13: 978-0-8272-0237-5
1. Church year. 2. Church year—Prayer-books and devotions—
English. 3. Church year meditations. I. Title.
  BV30.F67 2007
  264—dc22   2006033393

Printed in the United States of America

Contents

Acknowledgments

This book could never have been written without the encouragement and assistance of Trent Butler of Chalice Press. I owe him thanks beyond measure.

My sincere appreciation is extended to Rev. Chuck Sidoti, chaplain at South Pointe Hospital, Cleveland, Ohio, for his guidance in writing the "Blessing of the Hands Service"; Rev. Amos Acree, minister of East Aurora Christian Church (Disciples of Christ) in East Aurora, New York, for his guidance in preparing "The Alternate Service"; and to Rev. John Albert Gran, senior minister of First Christian Church, McPherson, Kansas, for use of material in an installation service. Thanks also go out to Ms. Mimi Weaver, Director of Development, Richmond Hill, Richmond, Virginia, for the use of her meditation and to the Rev. Dr. Chris Hobgood , a longtime friend and past interim General Minister of the Christian Church (Disciples of Christ) for his communion prayers. Thanks are also due to Marilyn Bolen for her assistance with the international breads and Linda Wilson for her assistance with the Maundy Thursday dinners.

Special thanks are expressed to those whose material was used in any way. Every effort has been made to identify and give proper credit. To the unknown authors, contributors, and original sources my thanks, and where appropriate my apologies for not being able to credit the source. Every effort will be made to correct in future editions. To them and to the authors designated as unknown, I express my heartfelt thanks.

Introduction

Special days are observed by the church to call us to remember the life of Jesus Christ and his command to go forth and serve. This memory of Jesus is renewed and revitalized as we participate through the year in observances centering around his birth, death, resurrection, and ministry.

Over the years I have seen these special days come and go. Sometimes they were observed in such a powerful way that individuals looked forward to the celebration with great anticipation. I have also seen days come and go with little care and/or significance. Perhaps this happened because individuals were called upon to lead at the last minute or with little guidance or available resources.

The material you now hold in your hands has been written carefully and prayerfully with the hope that it will be useful for many different groups: church school teachers and leaders; women's, men's and youth fellowships; elders, choirs, and lay leaders who serve on church boards, committees, or special focus groups such as outreach and missions; and those who serve as leaders of children, youth, and in intergenerational ministries.

Ministers will find helpful material for special occasions such as baptism, dedication and installation of elders, Maundy Thursday services, meditations for communion, and alternate worship services, and will also discover prayers for use with those who are ill or bereaved.

These resources may also be helpful for those called on to lead devotions for an event outside the church family such as a civic club meeting, school function, or an ecumenical gathering. Whatever the occasion or event, they are provided for your use in whatever way best fills your need.

My prayer is that they will enhance each of our ministries as we seek to follow Christ's command "to go and make disciples."

Dorothy D. France

Meditations
for the
Church Year

*A*DVENT _____

Advent, sometimes referred to as "Winter Lent," is the season that begins the church year in preparation for the celebration of the nativity of Christ. The word advent means "coming to" and refers to God's coming to humankind through the birth of Jesus Christ.

Let Every Heart Prepare Him Room[1]

Christ comes to all kinds of people. The Christmas story tells us that the first visitors to greet him from the outside were shepherds and "wise men." Here we have the humblest persons on one hand, and the most learned on the other.

Throughout his ministry Jesus met people in unusual places: Matthew at the seat of customs, Peter on the fishing boat, Mary and Martha in their home, the blind man by the side of the road, the woman in the crowd who touched the hem of his garment, the woman at the well, Zacchaeus in a sycamore tree, the money changers in the temple. He spent time with people involved in everyday tasks of life, and so it is with those of us who follow him today.

Christ will come this Christmas, as he does every day, to those who do the menial tasks of life, as the shepherds did, and to those who possess the highest intelligence and skills, as represented by the wise men. None of us, however, will be totally prepared to welcome him until we rise above the weariness incurred in preparation and the smallness that allows us to believe that he comes only to those like us, whether we tend the sheep or serve in the highest places of government.

Leo Tolstoy's story "Where Love Is, God Is" tells of a cobbler who looked for the coming of Christ into his shop. All day he watched. He saw a woman who needed food, so he shared his food with her. A boy entered who needed help, so he gave him assistance. Someone was cold, and the cobbler gave him the warmth of his stove. In the evening the cobbler wept because Christ had not come. It was then that he heard a voice that convinced him that Christ had indeed visited his shop. He was there with the woman who needed food, the boy who needed compassion, and the shivering man who warmed himself by the stove.

Christ came to me in a refugee camp on the island of Pulau Bidong off the coast of Malaysia. The island, which is mainly rock, was developed by the Malaysian Red Crescent and the government of Malaysia as a safe haven for the thousands of refugees who risked their lives in rickety old boats to find freedom wherever they could. If they were lucky and pushed off from the right spot at the right time of day when the current was just right, they would wash ashore onto this once barren island.

As my Church World Service colleagues, two Immigration and Naturalization Services (INS) representatives, and I approached the island in a government boat, we could see a large church and a Buddhist temple sitting at the top of a hill. It had been designated as "Religion Hill." Later the Commandant told us that those who developed the camp felt that it was important for refugees who had lost everything to have a place of worship if they were to survive.

We were fortunate to be on the island the evening that the newly formed Protestant church was meeting. It was just beginning to get dark as we followed our guide up a narrow path that led to the top. Following a period of refreshment, we joined our hosts in worship. Much to our surprise, we were given booklets containing Christmas carols printed in English. Ordinarily this might not have been so unusual; but this was mid-July, and we were in a refugee camp in Malaysia! They sang with such enthusiasm.

Soon it was time to go back down the hill. It was now pitch dark! Only a few of the leaders and refugees had flashlights—"torches" they called them. Those of us without them measured each step down that narrow rocky path as we tried to catch a little of the reflected light. About halfway down, a seven-year-old Vietnamese boy came up beside me, placed his hand on my elbow, and said in broken English, "Here, ma'am, I will share my light with you!"

Bethlehem was a busy, crowded town that night when Jesus was born. The people of Bethlehem were not necessarily hostile people. But they were busy. With great throngs pressing into town, requiring and often demanding attention, every place of lodging was filled. Apparently Joseph and Mary had not made reservations, much less guaranteed them for six o'clock arrival. But an innkeeper did offer his stable.

At the inn they may not have guessed who he was, but we have no such excuse. We know Jesus. The little Vietnamese boy hadn't known Jesus very long, but he understood the meaning of his coming. He was willing to share his light with a stranger.

Prayer: You have visited us on many occasions, O Lord, and found no room because our lives were overcrowded with meaningless hurrying and preoccupation with the unimportant. Try us again just now. We have prepared room for you. Amen.

PEACE SUNDAY

On the second Sunday of Advent congregations are encouraged to focus worship and study on the call from the Prince of Peace to be peacemakers.

Where Does Peace Begin?

On the altar in the Chapel of the Church Center for the United Nations in New York City are these words: "Would that even today you knew the things that make for peace." Too seldom do we think about our part in building a world at peace.

Several members from refugee resettlement offices were visiting camps located in Hong Kong, Thailand, Malaysia, and the Philippines. While visiting in Thailand, we were driven to a field hospital located on the Thai/Cambodian border. Ambulances were stationed at various points along the border, ready to bring injured soldiers as well as civilians to the field hospital operated by the organization "Doctors Without Borders." Volunteer doctors and nurses from the Netherlands were there to care for those who had sustained injuries from either gunfire or land mines.

As we neared the hospital complex, we tried to prepare ourselves for what we would experience in the next few hours. The administrator painted a dismal picture of what we would see. He wanted to make sure that we were ready emotionally to visit with some of those being treated.

We were told that we would not see the typical injuries resulting from gunfire, but rather the tragic maiming caused by land mines. Those mines, he told us, were no respecter of persons; they injured military and civilians, men and women, adults and children.

We each thought we had prepared ourselves for what we would encounter, but no amount of preparation could ease the pain of seeing helpless human beings as they lay on cots in a drab, sparsely furnished hospital unit.

One man had suffered multiple injuries, including the loss of both eyes. At the far end of the room lay a young woman whose leg had been blown off when she stepped on a land mine in a rice paddy. Her small child was sitting on a mat beside her cot, too young to understand the atrocities of war, but old enough to know that something horrible had happened to her mother.

As I stood beside that cot, I realized how little I really knew about war and how far removed my life had been from the human suffering caused by conflict around the world. As I view the reports of current discord, I try to understand; but I realize that I am still far removed from the pain of those immersed in the strife.

Jesus said: "Blessed are the peacemakers." He reminds us that we are to be just that, peacemakers, not peace*keepers* or those who dream of peace. What is the basic role of a peacemaker? Is it not to become a reconciler?

Each of us knows where we must begin. The words of Thomas á Kempis say it all: "First keep peace within yourself, then you can bring peace to others."[2] We often sing the hymn "Let there be peace on earth and let it begin with me." That's where it begins. It begins within our hearts as we relate more kindly with those we see at the grocery store, in a restaurant, at the mall, at our places of work, in our schools, or wherever we come in contact with others. It costs us nothing to reach out as we share a smile or lend a helping hand. We can teach our children and grandchildren not to shun those whose skin color is different or whose speech and customs seem unfamiliar.

Prayer: Dear God, we know that the dove of peace still finds the world covered with hatred and jealousy. We also know that as your followers our hearts may not always be at peace. We acknowledge that at times we have not been peacemakers; keeping the peace seemed so much easier. Help us to be more aware of the injustices that exist right where we live. Guide our thoughts and actions that, as we live more peaceably within our homes, our churches, and our communities, we may share in restoring and spreading your peace. Amen.

CHRISTMAS SUNDAY _____

Tradition says that the date of December 25 was established by Pope Julius I in the first half of the fourth century. The first celebration of December 25 as Christmas took place in Rome about 325 C.E. The word Christmas is really two words, Christ and mass. Mass comes from the same root as mission. God sent Jesus into the world so the world might be saved through him (Jn. 3:17). This was his mission. It was Christ's mass, thus Christmas.

Fear Not Little Flock

I have come to realize lately that I am a collector; a collector of thoughts—especially those from friends. Try as I may to discard notes passed to me during a meeting or handed to me by someone as they exit from worship, I want to hold onto them. They could be typed and filed away in my computer or on an index card, but somehow I want to keep them just the way they are. I want to keep them because they are in the individual's own handwriting. The ink may be faded with time, but it somehow enables me to stay in touch with someone or something that was once dear. I find it equally as hard to discard comments or commentary written in a newsletter or periodical by someone who has been a part of my life. I want to hold onto those reminders of the past.

Perhaps we all have a tendency to want to do that as Christmas draws near. We never seem to have enough time to prepare our home or our place of worship, let alone our heart. We open up those boxes containing handmade ornaments, a crèche inherited from a parent or grandparent, or something given to us by a special friend. We somehow feel in touch with those individuals.

In a box of Christmas items, I found a folder containing, among other trivia, the front page of a periodical dated December 1950. On the page was an article entitled "Christmas Has a Message," written by Dr. John A. Tate, one of the first persons to encourage me in ministry. With a few minor changes, such as location and mode of transportation—and a little editorializing—it could have been written yesterday.

"Tonight the news is depressing. The tide has turned in the fight for freedom in Korea. Our loved ones will not be home for Christmas. A global catastrophe seems inevitable. Man's inhumanity to man hasn't seemed to change much over the years. The night is dark and gloomy. Rain streams down the window of the Pullman car. Loneliness oppresses. Home may be momentarily farther behind. Weariness weights down. The load has been heavy, and still a time of facing grave problems is ahead. Tired in body and soul; distraught by fear; heavy of heart—small wonder the light of hope flickers with threatening extinction. The night is truly dark, and home is far.

"The rain rushes on into the ebon night. Then the brakes set. The mighty mechanism slows to a begrudged stop in a small town. The lifted shade lets in multicolored lights from the streets that remind that Christmas is near. It is Christmas week, and soft light filters through the darkness from yonder sanctuary where humble people worship.

"Imagination breaks the spell of depression. Children's faces are envisioned, alight with angelic fervor as the chorus sings, 'Silent Night, Holy Night.' The angel of God speaks again: 'Be of good cheer; I bring you good news of great joy.' Again to another, 'Jesus, the Savior is born.' The dispirited spell passes. The night is no longer dark, for hope has broken despair."

And it is ever so. Perhaps one conflict has been resolved, but others are building somewhere close to home or far away in a seemingly distant land. In one way or another many are still tired in body and soul, distraught by fear, heavy of heart. Is it any wonder that the light of hope flickers with threatening extinction? The night is truly dark.

All was not well in the little town of Bethlehem. It was crowded that night with people. "Everyone went to be registered, everyone to his own city." No doubt the night seemed dark for them too. Would they arrive in time? Would they have enough to tide them over until they returned home? Would they find lodging?

Let us go slow in thinking harsh thoughts of the Bethlehem innkeeper unless we have made a place in our heart and home for him. The highways and malls of our towns and cities are also crowded with travelers and shoppers hastening about to get those unfinished tasks completed. We reason that there must be a couple of bargains left as we search for that last-minute gift.

Christmas with all its beauty and significance must and will be kept this year. It will be kept even beneath the pall of dread and fear and despair wherever it enshrouds this world. It must be kept, for it is imperative to break the bonds of hopelessness. A Savior is born. The Child of Bethlehem is the Prince of Peace!

Christ speaks again: "Fear not, little flock, for it is your Father's good pleasure to give you the kingdom, to bring you hope, to bring you hope and peace." (Lk. 12:32 adapted)

Prayer: "O holy Child of Bethlehem, descend to us we pray; cast out our sin, and enter in; be born is us today."[3] Amen.

EPIPHANY

Tradition says the wise men arrived in Bethlehem on January 6. This day has been celebrated for hundreds of years as Epiphany, the manifestation to the Gentiles. In recent years there has been considerable interest in the twelve days of Christmas. The season is climaxed on the Twelfth Night by churches who organize festivities, often with neighborhood groups, to provide gifts to those most in need in their community.

God Used a Star

People always have watched the stars at night. Sitting around campfires, they often told stories of pictures the stars seemed to make in the skies. They gave names to some of the groups of stars, names we still use today: Orion, the Milky Way, the Big Dipper. The Arabs used one of the smallest stars in the Big Dipper to test their eyesight.

As individuals watched the stars night after night, and year after year, they learned how dependable they were, always appearing in a certain spot in the sky at a certain time of the month, in a certain month of the year. Long before people had clocks or calendars, they used the stars to guide them on their journeys. The darker the night, the brighter the stars seemed to shine.

God used a star to guide the wise men in their search for the King.

Then Herod summoned the wise men secretly and ascertained from them what time the star appeared; and he sent them to Bethlehem, saying, "Go and search diligently for the child, and when you have found him bring me word, that I too may come and worship him." When they had heard the king they went their way; and lo, the star which they had seen

in the East went before them, till it came to rest over
the place where the child was. (Mt. 2:7–9)

It was a dark night indeed when Mary bore Jesus. It was
a dark time for the nation, occupied by Romans. It was a dark
time for individuals too. Into that ever-deepening darkness, a
star shone over where the child lay, and the light of the world
began to shine.

*Prayer: Amid the world's darkness, O God, we seek the light of the
Bethlehem star to guide us and provide hope for the days that lie
ahead. Amen.*

WEEK OF PRAYER FOR CHRISTIAN UNITY

A worldwide observance, the annual Week of Prayer for Christian Unity began in the Episcopal Church in 1908 at Graymoor, in New York's Hudson Valley. The original Christian Unity Week began on the Feast of the Chair of Peter (at that time January 18) and ended on the Feast of the Church Unity Octave, since there were eight days between the two feasts. In 1935 Abbe Paul Couturier, a Catholic priest in France, advocated a "Universal Week of Prayer for Christian Unity" during which Christians would pray together "for the unity Christ wills by the means He wills." Over the years, with the encouragement of the National Council of Churches, many Christians have joined together to celebrate the Week of Prayer for Christian Unity.

Build a Bridge, Not a Wall

Shortly after the Second Vatican Council of the Roman Catholic Church (1962—1965), a woman of the Catholic faith presented a banner to an Assembly of Church Women United. At that time the majority of those in attendance were of the Protestant faith. The banner portrayed a wall being torn down and a bridge being erected in its place. Its message: "Build a Bridge, Not a Wall."

As she made her presentation, she pledged to build bridges of understanding among other religious groups, other races and nationalities. Where once there were walls, there must now be bridges, she said." For those present the dialogue in Protestant-Catholic relations began!

Each month I await the arrival of *Update*, the newsletter of Richmond Hill. This ecumenical Christian fellowship and residential community serves as stewards of an urban retreat center within the setting of a historic monastery located in

Richmond, Virginia. Their mission is to advance God's healing of metropolitan Richmond through prayer, hospitality, racial reconciliation, and spiritual development.

Mimi Weaver, director of development, writes an article each month under the heading: "Expanding the Circle." One of those articles, "Building Bridges," brought back pleasant memories of crossing the "nickel bridge" when I was a child. I knew several ways to get from my hometown to Richmond, but the shortest way was to cross the James River over the toll bridge. The toll was only a nickel. I was very young, but I remember leaning out the window to insert the coin while being held tightly by my older brother. When the coin was deposited, a clucking or clicking sound could be heard. As I reminisce, I consider that it doesn't take much else to excite a child if you have a river, a bridge, and a nickel. But God can help make big what was once small.

Ms. Weaver writes: " It is something of a joke among Richmond natives about crossing over our river…The James represents a clear boundary between 'us' and 'them.' The presence of the river makes the other side seem much further than it really is. Some would prefer to go a much further distance to find what they need just to keep from going across."

She continues: "Bridges can be scary, suspended high above rushing water and rocks. You make yourself vulnerable when you cross a bridge, and even more vulnerable when you build one. I guess that's the nature of bridges. It's no wonder we like to stay on our side of the river. But the view from the bridge is beautiful. Isn't it worth the risk?"[4]

Prayer: Forgive us, O God, for our walls of isolation, for our doors closed to others' needs. There have been iron and bamboo curtains, the Berlin wall, and our own fences. Forgive us for our selfish circles of love that keep others in their proper places and us secure in ours. Help us to be mindful of our bridges of faith that can unite us with those here at home and in other lands. Help us to demonstrate the unity of Christ not only in our prayers, but in our deeds of love and mercy. Guide us that we may learn to "build a bridge and not a wall." We pray in the name of the one who made us one family when he taught us to pray "Our Father." Amen.

LAITY SUNDAY

Laity Sunday combines the emphasis on the service of both men and women in the church. Woman's Day in the Christian Church (Disciples of Christ) was first observed on July 6, 1890, as National Christian Woman's Board of Mission Day. In 1920 the name was changed to Woman's Missionary Day, and then in 1936 it was changed to Woman's Day. Some congregations continue to observe the day under that name. Layman's Sunday was first observed by many churches as Men and Missions Sunday, which was established in the 1930s by the Laymen's Missionary Movement. United Church Men, the laymen's organization of the National Council of Churches, was established in 1950. Laymen's Sunday was formally inaugurated on October 19, 1952. The days were later combined to more accurately represent the work of both laymen and laywomen.

An Angel in the Rock

An age-old story pictures Michelangelo struggling to push a boulder up a hill to his home. Then he began furiously pounding on the rock with his sculpting tools. A curious bystander asked why he labored so over an "old piece of rock." Michelangelo is reported to have answered, "Because there is an angel in the rock waiting to come out."

Many of us go through life with little thought of what our role is really worth; we are always in a hurry. Seldom do we sit down and take the time to evaluate what is taking place as we go along. We hesitate to become involved in what may be a very worthwhile activity because we are already so busy. Yet God has something special inside that God wants to bring out if we will just stop and let the divine Sculptor chisel away at our lives.

Many years ago when I was a young minister's wife, I attended a luncheon for clergy spouses at a General Assembly of the Christian Church. The speaker gave sound advice that has served as a guideline for me over the years. Her advice: "You must learn to choose in order that you will go about doing good rather than just going about." In other words, be mindful of how you are spending your life. Make each moment count! Acknowledge that you can make a contribution and bring something to another's life that no one but you can bring. You are unique!

The Dunet family arrived in the United States as refugees from Kiev, Ukraine, in late 1989. Though all the families resettled through the Virginia Church World Service office were special to me, this one was extra-special because the family of three had been sponsored by the church with which my husband and I were affiliated.

Several years after the family's arrival, I could count on having a brief conversation with Roman, the father, every Sunday. He had been an artist and had studied at the Kiev Institute of Fine Arts. He would continue to be employed, however, as the sexton at the sponsoring church until such time as he became fluent in English and acclimated in his new work environment. In the meantime he continued to paint, hoping that one day he would be ready to earn his living as an artist.

One Sunday morning prior to the beginning of church school, Roman said hello to me as he always did. But on this particular morning he greeted me, handed me a cup of coffee, and then said, "I need to ask you a question. There is something I don't understand." When I asked him what he didn't understand, he replied: "When someone asks me, 'How are you?' is it just a greeting or do they really want to know how I am?"

"What do you think it means?" I asked. "I think it must be just a greeting," he said. "When I begin to tell someone how I am and what I have been learning, the person just nods and walks away. In the Ukraine," he continued, "a person who asks an individual how he or she is really wants to know, not just about the individual, but about the family as well. That's one of the things I miss most about my country."

We talked a while longer, and I realized that I was going to be really late for my class. But the words of advice I had received long ago came flashing through my brain reminding me that just maybe being on time for my class would just be "going about." Taking time to help make life a little easier for someone like Roman just might be "going about doing good."

Someone said that God gives us the raw materials; we have to do something with them. I have always admired a friend who could clip a few branches from a flowering shrub, several jonquils from her flowerbed, and several pieces from the potted fern sitting on her porch and create an arrangement of beauty. What amazed me the most is that she would do this just before leaving for a visit to someone who was confined to a nursing facility. She wanted the flowers to be fresh for the one who once was able to maintain her own flower garden.

Isn't it amazing how much God needs each of us? He needs each and every one of us to be his heart, hands, and feet as we go about doing good.

I read
In a book
That a man called
CHRIST
Went about doing good.
It is very disconcerting to me
That I am so easily
Satisfied
With just going about.[5]

Prayer: O Lord, help me to be the angel in the rock waiting to come out and provide assistance to others. Keep me ever mindful of how swiftly life can be spent. Help me to make each moment count. In the name of my serving Savior I offer this prayer. Amen.

RACE RELATIONS SUNDAY

The first observance of Race Relations Sunday was on February 11, 1923. Today the observance is a time when churches are encouraged to give attention to programs and activities that will improve race relations. The day provides an excellent opportunity for all racial groups to learn more about the racial and cultural backgrounds of persons living in their communities.

Waving Isn't Enough

The real beauty of my neighborhood became apparent as I opened my door to give treats to the children one Halloween. They came in all sizes and colors holding open their containers—bags, pumpkins, hats, and even pillowcases. Some stood quietly with patience while others literally screamed out, "Trick or Treat!" When the evening was over, I felt that I had opened my door to a miniature United Nations delegation. My visitors included Japanese, Chinese, Vietnamese, Lebanese, Indian, German, and African American children, all with their parents waiting close by.

Did I know them? Yes and no. I knew they lived in the neighborhood; we waved to each other, especially in the summertime. I didn't appreciate what they meant to me until that night when I saw the faces of the children. Some lifted their masks when I handed them their treats, and occasionally one would say, "It's me!" Since that evening I have discovered that the better acquainted I become with those of different cultures and racial groups, the more I realize that the desires, aspirations, and capabilities of all people are much the same.

A Romanian father who entered the United States with his family as refugees made this comment to his sponsor: "We are so grateful and blessed to be here. We know that in America we have the opportunity to provide a wonderful future for our children." For that to become a reality we must go beyond waving and handing out treats; we all must learn to join hands in friendship and support.

Someone once wrote that Jesus, the revealer of God, looks like us. We may meet him many times each day, but we may not recognize him because of the clothing he is wearing or the color of his skin or the station in life he occupies. Many of us will miss him if we are looking for a halo or a robe or racial excellence. Jesus walks wherever an individual bears the load of another, wherever the strong-hearted fight against injustice, wherever in the limelight or in the shadows and alone people are true to their faith and keep their covenant with God.

We confess that while we have grown more caring in some ways, we have become more callous in others. Our love is often too cautious, too calculating. It is easier for us to give God lip service while we are in worship, but the real test of our devotion to him is the approach we take to our neighbors.

Walk together, talk together O ye people of the earth;
Then and only then shall you have peace.

SANSKRIT

Prayer: O, Lord, creator and sustainer of all, accept our thanks for the variety reflected in the color and tint of our skin and for the beauty and the value of each and every personality. Help us to count as equals all members of the human family, that we may truly do honor to you who made us in your own image. Amen.

WEEK OF COMPASSION

Week of Compassion is a special outreach offering period for the Christian Church (Disciples of Christ) world relief, rehabilitation, and development ministries. It is generally observed the third week in February. Many other denominations observe this time as One Great Hour of Sharing. The first Week of Compassion was held in 1944.

May Your Heart Remain Moist

"The head does not hear until the heart has listened." A friend handed me a small piece of paper containing these words during a Bible study session. Over the years I have transferred the words from one business card to another and then to another whenever the edges became tattered. They remind me that hearing is not enough. My heart must learn to listen!

On the island of La Gonave, a barren outcropping in Port-au-Prince Bay, Haiti, my colleagues and I visited the site of the only source of water, located some three hours by foot from most of the islanders' houses. The women and small children walked three hours out and three hours back each day to obtain a plastic bucket or bottle of water.

They stood patiently in line and chatted with each other like we used to talk with our neighbors over the back fence. They considered it an additional blessing if they could find a few leaves from whatever was still growing to place on top of the water to keep it from splashing out as they walked back to their homes.

The night before, I had used the shower stall located just outside the back door of the home where I was staying. It seemed like half the neighborhood was preparing dinner over an open fire in the backyard. A curtain gave me privacy except for my head and feet. It was a little embarrassing, but

I showered as they occasionally looked up at me. I'm sure the shower cap on my head and the flip-flops on my feet made interesting conversation. In that home I experienced firsthand what it was like to be without the modern conveniences we take for granted. The shower was a bucket of water rigged on a pipe. When you pulled the cord, the bucket emptied, and that ended the shower. One bucket was all they had for that day, and they had saved it for me! I kept thinking. "I am here only one night, but they are here for their lifetime!"

The next day was another long day, and my legs and feet were tired from going up and down the hillsides as we continued to visit wells in neighboring Dominican Republic. All of the wells were made possible through money raised in walks for the hungry in other countries. We arrived at the location of our last visit for the day. As we began to follow a narrow rugged path to descend the steep hill, I suggested to my colleagues that they go ahead. I would sit on a nearby rock and make notes of the day's events while they descended further to the well site.

I was deep in thought when I heard the voice of the man standing beside the well: "Hey, lady. Hey, lady. Come see." I waved and then reluctantly made my way to the bottom of the hill. As I stood on tiptoe trying to look over the wall of the well, the young Dominican, placed his hands on my waist, lifted me up so I could peer down into the well and said, "See lady, living water! See lady, living water." To me the wells all looked alike, but to him this was the one that brought life-giving water to the people in his village.

Most of us don't worry about water. We turn on the faucet, and there it is. It is there to drink when we are thirsty; to prepare food when we are hungry; to use in preparing tea or coffee to share with a friend; to shower or take a bath whenever we choose; or to do the laundry, wash the car, or water the garden. It's just something that is available whenever we need it.

Recently we have added a new dimension to our "thing" about water. If the tap water doesn't taste to our liking, we hasten to get it in bottled form. We attach it to our belt or place it in our purse or pocket so we can take a sip wherever or whenever we wish. Yet, in many other areas of the world, water continues to be a precious commodity, one that must never be wasted. Individuals savor the very last drop that touches their parched lips. It is a precious resource for personal use but also necessary to grow the food on which life depends.

Devastating hurricanes and tsunamis reminded us once again of how necessary fresh water is for all of life. The people stranded in New Orleans needed fresh, noncontaminated water in order to survive, and some did not get it in time.

Water is a gift. It is truly one of the miracles of God.

"And whoever gives to one of these little ones even a cup of cold water...he shall not lose his reward." (Mt. 10:42)

Prayer: O Lord, help us keep our hearts moist with compassion as we share living water. Amen.

ASH WEDNESDAY

    Ash Wednesday is the first day of Lent, the fortieth weekday before Easter. It received its name from the practice of marking or rubbing the forehead of the penitent and, later, all the faithful with ashes. The ceremony was an ancient sign of mourning. When the time and length of the Lenten season was set at forty days, it was appropriate that this season of denial and soul-searching should begin with this ritual.

    Many churches save the palm branches used on Palm Sunday. When they have been properly dried, they are burned to provide the ashes for use on Ash Wednesday the following year.

Angry Compassion

    The telephone rang. On the other end of the line was the chair of the committee charged with obtaining speakers for the district Lenten services. The committee had decided to ask the retired clergy to be the speakers. The theme was "Stones of Anger." My first reaction was, *Who wants to talk about anger? I don't. What would I say?* Nevertheless, I accepted the challenge.

    After I read and reread the assigned scripture, it became clear to me. I admitted for the first time that my "anger" at what I witnessed often changed the direction of my life. Events, happenings, and experiences change our lives! You may not realize it, but certain things have and will continue to change your life as well.

    Following 9/11, New York City experienced a power outage. One reporter overheard several people remark that without all the lights in Times Square they could really see the stars for the first time. That tragic event caused some folks to take the time to look up and see the brilliance of the stars. In an area in Port-au-Prince, Haiti, called "Brooklyn," I witnessed the worst poverty I had ever seen. The housing was horrible; the whole scene was beyond description. Dozens of people stood in line to fill plastic containers with water from the only spigot in the area. The air was thick with the pungent smell from the nearby open sewer.

"How can this be?" I asked myself. "How can this be in a country just a few hours from where I live?"

Later that evening I really felt angry; I wanted to cry out in despair. The members of our group were guests for an elaborate dinner in one of the posh hotels located only a fifteen-minute drive from the area where the poorest of the poor lived. As we departed the restaurant that night, we walked—I should say, we were *escorted*—through the gambling casino frequented by the rich and famous from around the world. Many were Americans; we could tell by their accents. They were dressed in their finest party attire.

We paused inside the doorway at one end of the casino. As I scanned the large room, I recalled the scripture: "And Jesus entered the temple of God and drove out all who sold and bought in the temple, and he overturned the tables of the money-changers and the seats of those who sold pigeons" (Mt. 21:12). I could see Jesus overturning those tables like dominos. He was very angry as he said—no, *screamed* out—to them: "It is written, 'My house shall be called a house of prayer'; but you make it a den of robbers"(Mt. 21:13).

What is anger? What does it mean to be angry?

Anger is an English word translated from an Old Norse word *angr,* said to mean "trouble, affliction, even feeling pain." Someone has said that anger is an addiction, a poison. *Webster's Collegiate Dictionary* defines *anger* as, "A strong passion or emotion of displeasure which is usually excited by a sense of injury or insult." Anger sometimes shows itself as resentment, disappointment, and impatience. Some synonyms for *anger* are *rage, fury, indignation,* and *brokenness.* Words that include the word *anger* include *danger, dangerous,* and *stranger.* Maybe you can think of others.

As we join in worship, are you angry with anyone or about anything? Perhaps you are angry because of the loss of a job or the fear of being transferred. Maybe you are frustrated over having to change or make an unexpected move. Are you angry because of the loss of a family member, friend, or pet? Or, are you angry because of something someone said to or about you that wasn't true? Perhaps you are tired of wars and rumors of wars that seem only to harm others and in the end threaten us. Perhaps you're angry with a neighbor because his yard isn't trimmed the way you think it should be. Or maybe you are really angry or hurt because no matter how hard you try at work, at home, or at church your feelings or opinions don't seem to matter.

Over the years I have learned that anger can be both good and bad. It can cause an ulcer or make a pearl. How we handle it is what counts. Robert A. F. Thurman in his book *Anger* writes, "Anger is never pacified by anger. It is pacified by love. This is the eternal truth. To stop anger you can't be angry."[6] Ash Wednesday and the season of Lent can be a time for new beginnings, a time of releasing and transforming the anger in our lives into something special.

> "For everything there is a season and a time for every matter under heaven:…a time to cast away stones, and a time to gather stones together." (Eccl. 3:1, 5a)

When Jesus overturned the money-changers' tables in the temple, he was very angry, but his anger was driven by compassion. "And the blind and the lame came to him in the temple, and he healed them" (Mt. 21:14). A friend of mine calls this "angry compassion."

When God gets us completely alone by sickness, afflic-tion, disappointment, heartbreak, or a broken friendship, he becomes real to us; and things happen. God does not and will not take away trials or carry us over them, but he will through the love of his son, Jesus Christ, strengthen us so we can get through them.

We can learn through his guidance that anger can be transformed into a compassion that will enable us to join with others in making right some of the wrongs in our lives and society. We can then bring something positive out of what seems at the present time to be all negative.

As we worship and receive the ashes, now is a perfect time for each of us to remember that no matter where we live, we are "one body in Christ." Grace Bunker, recently retired missionary from Sri Lanka, says, "We are doing together what cannot be done alone."

"And Jesus entered the temple of God and drove out all who sold bought in the temple, and he overturned the tables of the money-changers and the seats of those who sold pigeons" (Mt. 21:12)—he was angry!

"And the blind and the lame came to him in the temple, and he healed them" (Mt. 21:14)—he showed compassion!

Prayer: Almighty and merciful God, we ask that you temper our anger with love and compassion. Help us to understand that only by living a life of love and service can we truly follow your example of sacrifice. Amen.

LENT

The Western Church has observed Lent, the annual season of fasting, prayer, penitence, and spiritual examination since the first century after Christ. The six Sundays are not considered a part of Lent. In the Western Church, Sunday is always a feast day. The forty weekdays following Ash Wednesday and ending at noon on the Saturday of Holy Week constitute Lent. The word Lent comes from the Anglo-Saxon word for Spring, which is derived from a verb meaning "to lengthen."

A Spiritual Heart Transplant

The two-hour flight from Bangkok to the smaller city of Chiangmai, Thailand, was basically without incident. Although the plane was smaller and lacked some of the comforts of the larger carriers, we managed to keep our composure for most of the flight. We remained relatively calm by keeping our thoughts and conversation focused on the new experiences that lay ahead.

We arrived safely and learned at the conclusion of a brief orientation that we would be joining several local women in their weekly visit to the women's prison. Many young girls had migrated to the city from their rural homes in search of employment and, hopefully, a more fulfilling life. Unable to find jobs, they had turned to prostitution and stealing to survive. Some ended up in trouble with the law and eventually were imprisoned. The women's fellowship had become concerned about these young girls and visited each week not only to share a time of fellowship but also to share with them the church's message of hope found in Jesus Christ.

It seemed strange, then, and still does today, that my first visit with women in prison would take place thousands of miles away from home. As I sat there on the mat that partially covered the dirt floor, I wondered what could and would be shared with these young women during the time of devotions. After introductions were made and refreshments served, one of the women took a small sheet of cardboard from the cloth in which it had been wrapped. On one side I could see an advertisement for some local product. On the other side I noticed that she had drawn a simple stick figure of a woman with her face penciled in and a red heart drawn on her chest.

The woman held up her "poster" so all could see and then began her message. I will never forget what she said. "We learned recently that in a country very far away, a country called South Africa, a doctor performed the first heart transplant. He was able to take the heart from a man who was dying and place it in the body of another man that he might live. We cannot or do not need to do that for you. We do want to tell you about a man called Jesus who can give you a heart transplant. He will not remove your heart from your body, but he can take all of the bad things, all the things that you have done wrong in your life, and replace them with love and kindness. He can transform your life if you believe."

I was moved to tears as I sat listening. I once visited the Groote Schuur Hospital in Cape Town, South Africa, where Dr. Christiaan Barnard, the noted heart surgeon, made medical history by transplanting the heart of a black man into the chest of a white man. As I listened, I recalled how surprised I was that this amazing surgery had taken place in a very small hospital that was less equipped than the modern medical facilities with which I was familiar. Now here in this small women's prison I was listening as my Thai sister shared not only the miracle that had taken place in South Africa but also the miracle of healing and forgiveness that takes place daily through the love of Jesus Christ and the church throughout the world.

Dr. Barnard tells in one of his books about admitting an eight-year-old girl, whom he had never met, to the hospital. When he went by the room to inquire about her condition and become acquainted, he asked, "Why did you come to me?" The little girl answered, "I have a broken heart!" Broken hearts still abound all over the world to this day. Some are emotionally or spiritually broken, while others are physically broken. Care comes to those whose hearts need to be replaced through organ transplant. Those whose hearts need mending are given care by the medical profession. Care comes spiritually as individuals work together in bringing love and hope.

> [H]e has sent me to bind up the brokenhearted,
> to proclaim liberty to the captives,
> and the opening of the prison
>   to those who are bound.* (Isa. 61:1b)

Prayer: During this season of Lent we come to you, Lord, acknowledging that we, too, have broken hearts. We come repenting of the things that have caused pain and anguish. We come seeking the healing and cleansing presence of a living Christ who gave his life that our hearts might be restored.

PALM SUNDAY

Palm Sunday is the last Sunday in Lent and the first day of Holy Week, which precedes Easter. As a Christian observance it dates back to about the tenth century. It commemorates the triumphal entry of Jesus into Jerusalem when the common people welcomed him by holding aloft branches of the palm tree (Jn. 12:13). The use of palm leaves on the anniversary dates back to the early period in the history of the Jerusalem church. It continues to be an appropriate symbol of peace.

Who Doesn't Love a Parade?

What a beautiful scene, with the waving of palm branches and the singing of "Hosannas." Jesus, during a time of personal danger and discord, came riding humbly and meekly into the holy city of Jerusalem upon a donkey. The crowd that surrounded him carried mixed emotions. Some adored him as they proclaimed him "king"; others were grateful for the influence he had on their lives. To be sure many came just to satisfy their curiosity and be in the midst of the crowd. It was a wonderful parade for many who lined the way.

Who is there among us who doesn't love a parade? We like being a part of the crowd, whether close up and personal or viewing from a distance. We enjoy the parades in our own communities with marching bands and floats featuring local celebrities who wave and toss flowers and candy to those along the way. We delay arriving on time for other commitments to be a part of the television specials with the amazing Thanksgiving and Rose Bowl parades that entertain both the young and the not-so-young. But the Palm Sunday procession was, is, and should be different!

Henri J. M. Nouwen wrote: "Without solitude it is virtually impossible to live a spiritual life…we often use outer

distractions to shield ourselves from the interior noises."[7]
If we are to feel, witness, and recognize his presence as we
join in declaring "Hosanna," some time needs to be spent in
preparation. Perhaps a period of silence and solitude would
be in order.

Jesus accepted their praises as he moved through the
crowd, knowing that it would soon be over. He did not
soften or change his challenge to the leaders; he did not try
to escape when he had the chance. He later allowed himself
to be arrested, tried, and crucified.

The scripture tells us: "And when they drew near to
Jerusalem, to Bethphage and Bethany, at the Mount of Olives,
he sent two of his disciples . . ." (Mk. 11:1). In our silence we
may read these words as, "And when he came near to my
hometown, he sent two of us…" Who among us will be ready
for the assignment?

Palm Sunday was for Jesus a time of heart-searching. In
every age those who would serve in his name are called on
to renew their mission in the face of the world's pressures
to compromise and accommodate. It is, for us, a time when
we are called upon to reaffirm the essentials and reorder the
priorities of our lives. Each year's observance of Palm Sunday
is a continuing reminder of this fact.

The hosannas that we shout when with the palm-waving
crowd must be more than the noises we make when cheering
for our favorite player or team. They must become for us a
commitment to the highest and the best that we can be. After
all, our shouts of "Hallelujah!" will amount to nothing unless
we are prepared and willing to recognize and follow Jesus.
Let us join in the procession with the crowd in Jerusalem
knowing that our search for salvation will continue as we
await his resurrection.

The church with psalms must shout,
No door can keep them out;
But, above all, the heart

Must bear the longest part.
Let all the world in every corner sing:
My God and King!

GEORGE HERBERT 1593—1633[8]

MAUNDY THURSDAY

The Thursday before Easter commemorates the institution of the Lord's supper, which Jesus initiated in the upper room with his disciples. The word maundy is derived from the Latin word mandatum, which means a commission, especially a verbal commission. It is associated with Jesus' command after the Last Supper, found in John 13:34: "A new commandment I give to you, that you love another."

Is It I, Lord?

To travel back over the country roads to places once held dear can be both challenging and rewarding—challenging because so much has changed, rewarding because so many objects bring back wonderful memories.

The church was picturesque as it sat pristine on a hill that somehow seemed much closer to town than it once did. It was springtime. The flowers were still being cared for with tender loving care. Inside, the smell of fresh paint was in the air. The choir loft was much larger, and an organ sat where the piano once reigned supreme. "That's progress!" I thought. The beautifully carved communion table sat front and center, where it always had. An educational wing and fellowship hall had been added. The nursery was painted with bright colors, and the room furnished with cribs and rocking chairs. The whole building was evidence that extended families continued to come to this special place for study and worship. The walls held pictures that portrayed the world of today, but also pictures that helped keep precious memories alive.

As I entered an adult classroom, my eyes were drawn to a copy of the painting *The Last Supper*. I recognized it as one that had been painted years ago by an elderly member from "a paint-by-number kit." A group of women would gather twice a month, sit around a table, catch up on the news, and try their hand at painting. Some used the kits, but others dreamed of moving on one day to being able to paint without a chart. Whenever I visited with them, I anticipated a continued discussion about that one painting. Do you think that "on that night" when Jesus gathered with his disciples for a meal, they all sat on one side of the table? Do you think that Jesus knowing what lay ahead of him would have commissioned an artist to paint a family portrait? The elderly artist always insisted that Jesus had more on his mind that night. After all, sitting with him was one who would betray him and one who would deny him. "Lord, is it I?" they asked.

Leonardo da Vinci, the Italian artist who painted *The Last Supper* in 1498, is said to have been the greatest genius who ever lived. Painting was only one of the many activities through which he displayed his talents. He was also a sculptor, an architect, an engineer, philosopher, writer, and musician. He designed the most remarkable bridges and warships of his day. He believed in solving the insolvable, and yet some remember him for this one painting.

Few scenes in the life of Christ have been painted more often than the Last Supper. There at the table is John the Beloved; impulsive Peter and Judas; Andrew, James the younger and Bartholomew; Thomas, James the elder and Philip; Matthew, Thaddeus, and Simeon. And there are you and I! Jesus was there and is here tonight. In Da Vinci's painting Jesus looks sad, submissive, and forgiving, as though he were hopeful that Judas might yet repent before it was too late.

Da Vinci painted the picture on the walls of a convent dining room in Milan, Italy. Seated at their meals, the brothers of the monastery could look on the table of Christ. Each time we join in worship, we are privileged to come to the table where Christ, the host, will welcome us. As we gather here this night, have we come to pose for a painting? Are we here to be seen by other followers, or are we here to ask, "Is it I, Lord?" Are we ready to accept the cup of sacrifice, or would we prefer just to receive the cup of blessing? Each of us will have to answer the question for ourselves and ourselves alone: "Is it I, Lord?"

Prayer: O Lord, forgive us for seeking your blessings but avoiding your suffering. We pray that our hearts may be large enough to comprehend the greatness of your sacrifice as well as the depths of your love. Amen.

EASTER

Easter is the Christian festival that annually celebrates the resurrection of Jesus Christ from the dead. The word Easter is derived from the name of the Teutonic goddess of spring, Eostre. The celebration of Easter as the feast of the resurrection was general among Christians by the end of the second century.

As the Day Began to Break

The Garden Tomb in Jerusalem will always be a special place. No other location in what we refer to as "the Holy Land" brings the sense of peace that is found there. I had always dreamed of being in that special garden at sunrise. At the Y.M.C.A. where we were staying, I asked about making an early morning visit to the garden and was told that the gate wasn't opened until much later in the morning. The director agreed to check with the caretaker to see if special arrangements could be made for us to visit. Later that evening when we returned, we found a note at the front desk. Arrangements had been made for a visit before daybreak the next morning. The caretaker, who lived at the garden, would open the gate at 5:30 a.m. We should lock it when we left. The note also said, "You will not be able to see the sun rise from here, but you will enjoy the dawn as the day begins to break."

That next morning, as we sat on the bench in the garden, we opened our New Testaments and read together briefly from each of the gospels: "Now after the sabbath, toward the dawn of the first day of the week…And very early on the first day of the week they went to the tomb when the sun had risen…But on the first day of the week, at early dawn…Now on the first day of the week Mary Magdalene came to the tomb early, while it was still dark" (Mt. 28:1a; Mk. 16:2; Lk. 24:1a; Jn.

20:1a). All those years I had gone to services at "sunrise" or to some that were held much later in the morning, I missed so much by not being there at the first break of day! Such peace. Such quiet. Such a marvelous time to join him. I now began to understand where Jesus had received his strength for his strenuous days of service. He had retreated to a quiet spot, such as a garden. There he could be alone and be refilled as the day began to break or the sun disappeared at nightfall.

"No night was ever so dark as the night before the first Easter morning: a darkness that had begun at noon on Calvary. The women started out on their journey to the tomb 'while it was still dark,' but as they went on their way with love and hope, it began to dawn,"[9] wrote the late Dr. Lin D. Cartwright.

We had arrived in the garden when it was dark; now as the day began to break, light overcame the darkness. Just before leaving, I took the only piece of paper I had in my purse and wrote my prayer:

> O gracious Father, you who gave your Son to be crucified for my sins and the sins of the world, enable me in this hour of quietness in this garden to capture the significance of his death, but more importantly to realize the significance and real meaning of his resurrection. Enable me like Mary to "go tell" all whom I meet about the Risen Lord. As the tolling of the bells now breaks the silence around me, may I be willing to break the silence of complacency, the silence of non-involvement, the silence of indifference. As Jesus broke the bonds of death, may I strive more earnestly to break the bondage of prejudice, hate, envy, greed, and self-satisfaction that keeps Jesus nailed to the cross. As each new day begins to break, may I rededicate my life to serving a Risen Lord in a world that so desperately needs his presence. Amen.

As we left the garden and fastened the lock on the gate, we could hear the roosters crowing in the distance as we walked back to the Y.M.C.A. What a wonderful beginning to a new day.

> Let the heavens be joyful
> Let earth her song begin…
> For Christ the Lord hath risen,
> Our joy that has no end.

JOHN OF DAMASCUS (676–749)

*EARTH STEWARDSHIP SUNDAY*_____

Earth Stewardship Sunday is celebrated on the Sunday following Earth Day, April 22. Congregations are encouraged to spend at least one week each year in study, action, and worship focused on environmental stewardship.

The Earth Is the Lord's

One hundred and twenty women from forty-two countries, with less than 20 percent from the United States, gathered for an International Consultation at Anderson College in Anderson, Indiana. It was planned as a time "of finding each other in the international community." Newsprint was used to record the brainstorming that took place during many of the sessions. Even when the smallest mistake was made, the whole page was removed and tossed into the trash. After all, neatness is a virtue! During one of the sessions, an international guest became upset and began to cry. What had upset her? It was the fact that so much paper was being wasted. She stated that paper was very scarce and expensive in her country; they cherished every scrap they could obtain.

Years ago my elementary school principal required the teachers to tear the paper towels in half before handing them to the children when they washed their hands. Today she would be encouraged if she walked into an airport restroom and saw that the towels in the dispensers were already halved. She would be pleased that after thirty years we were beginning to conserve.

Earl F. Barfoot, in an article on stewardship, tells of a brainstorming session with some youth who were working on a retreat agenda. He scribbled all kinds of notes on a sheet of newsprint but reached a point where words and phrases were all jumbling together. He tore off the paper and began writing on another sheet when he was interrupted by one of the youth. "Just a minute," the young man said, "You haven't used the other side of that paper. Don't waste it." Mr. Barfoot thought he was kidding and made a remark about using both sides of the napkin. But the young man was serious. He continued, "Do you know how many trees it takes to put out a daily newspaper? Do you know I took notes in my classes all year on the clean side of the paper my father was going to throw away?"

Many Christians have been concerned about the Earth and the environment for decades. Volumes have been written about our responsibility to be good stewards, and many people have responded. But we are rapidly becoming aware that, although the solutions are difficult, each of us must determine what our role can and will be. A newspaper article detailed the efforts of two women in Ohio who rode around their neighborhood or sometimes other neighborhoods picking up anything they thought could be used or sold from what others put out as trash. The women called their recycling activity "curbing." The article advised that the best time to "curb" is either late at night or early in the morning. For some it adds a little extra to the ever-popular yard sale circuit. Maybe the motive is cash and not recycling, but whatever the motive, every bit helps.

The article reminded me of a delightful woman who lived in a low-income apartment complex. Marcie checked through what others had discarded. She was very selective in what she gathered; the items had to be salvageable. She laundered and mended the clothing, sewed on buttons, and repaired zippers, all with tender loving care. When she had a bag or two of items, she brought them to the local Church World Service office to be used in the clothing drive. She didn't have money to give and was unable to work due to poor health, but she did have time, which she gladly gave so that others or their children would have clothing.

When will we learn, as Gandhi suggested, to live simply so that others may simply live? There may be no individual solution to the problem; yet the healing of our relationship with the earth ultimately needs to emerge from each of our hearts and our spirits.

> You shall be called the repairer of the breach,
>   the restorer of streets to dwell in. (Isa. 58:12b)

Prayer: O Lord, help us not to be careless and uncaring in the way we use the resources you have stored up in the earth. Help us to be good stewards that those who follow may see the beauty and share in the blessings of your creation. Amen.

CHRISTIAN FAMILY WEEK

Christian Family Week was inaugurated in 1942, the first full year of United State involvement in World War II. Many families and home ties were being uprooted. There came the realization that a nation, a society, and a church are only as strong as the families that make them up. Thus the family week observance began and has continued down to the present time. The observance, beginning on the first Sunday in May, leads up to Mother's Day.

A Group Hug

One Sunday morning just before church began, several teenage young men greeted me in their usual way as we met in the hall. We usually hugged each other, and one would ask, "What can we do to get into trouble today?" Then we would have a good laugh. Usually what they meant by getting in trouble was going to the fellowship hall to find something to eat.

On this particular morning, I said, "If we're going to get into trouble, we'd better have another group hug first." As we put our arms around each other, forming a circle, one of them said, "Let's don't call it a group hug. Let's huddle like you say in your football book."

When I arrived home, I retrieved a copy of the humorous little football book from my coffee table. My grandsons and I had written it together several years earlier; I wrote the humor, and they wrote the rules. I looked up "huddle" because I had forgotten what I had written.

It read: "You might be a football fan if you know that a Huddle is not what happens when a person wants to be alone."

On the back of the page, it said: "A huddle takes place when players get together in a group, usually forming a circle, to agree on the strategy and signal for the next play."[10]

Little did I realize that these youngsters and I had been following that rule for a long time as we greeted one another on Sunday mornings. I realized that maybe a "group hug," as I called it, had been filling a need, that the hug or the huddle was just the beginning of what could and should happen as we gathered as a church family. It began as we greeted each other on arrival, but continued as we went to our classes and to the sanctuary for worship. It was not an end in itself but a moment of realizing that, in Christ, whether we are young or old, we are never alone. We are family! We all need hugs sometime in our lives.

Today's families come in all sizes, shapes, and colors. Some families live in homes with parents and brothers and sisters, and maybe grandma, too. Others live in single-parent households, and still others live in what we sometimes call "blended" families. Some older persons consider the retirement community where they live their family. Some employees in companies who have worked together for a long time call themselves family. School children sometimes consider those in their class or in the choir or the band their family. Some neighborhood associations consider their neighbors as part of their family. We even occasionally talk about one day living as a family of nations.

Whoever we are and wherever we live, we all need to be linked together with someone or some group. There are times when we all want to feel the embrace of a group hug or huddle. It just feels good to be hugged.

Prayer: Help us, O Lord, to be kind to our family, those nearest us. But when we are unkind, help us to express love so that hurts can be healed. Amen.

PENTECOST

On Pentecost, the birthday of the Church, the first Christians, in obedience to Jesus, "were all together in one place." There they became one in experience and purpose with the gift of the Holy Spirit. This day, also called Whitsunday, comes fifty days after Easter and celebrates this gift.

Listen to the Wind

A storm was brewing. I knew that for sure as I flinched from the bright flashes of lightning and then the roar of thunder. I increased my speed, hoping I could get to the shopping center before the rains came. The lights of oncoming cars were now beaming toward me, another sign the storm was moving my way. If I made it, I reasoned, I could complete my shopping, have a snack, and return home without wasting any precious time.

I pulled into the parking lot with a sigh of relief. I made it! And then the winds came. Trash cans tumbled over. Bits of paper, leaves, and whatever else was in the storm's path went flying by. Then, there before me was a parking place right near the door. How lucky can you get? I quickly learned, though, that when the wind is blowing it makes its presence felt. It proved to be stronger than I was. No matter how hard I pushed, the door would not open.

Other folks were running across the parking lot; obviously, they had opened their doors. I finally moved the car so it would be facing in a different direction. This time the door yielded to my push. I had stopped trying to open the door against the wind. When I was safely inside, shopping completed and coffee in hand, I sat down to wait out the rain. I recalled the words of Jesus to Nicodemus, a Pharisee, and ruler of the Jews. I had just read them the night before, but now I heard them in a different way. "The wind blows where it wills, and you hear the sound of it, but you do not know whence it comes or whither it goes; so it is with every one who is born of the Spirit" (Jn. 3:8).

James S. Stewart, a Scottish minister, wrote: "So from the beginning of days to the last syllable of recorded time, the wind blows—the Spirit of God is at work…It is the Spirit that holds human life together. Never does He cease working. The wind blows." He continues: "The New Testament says that at one particular point of history there was a sudden new irruption of the Spirit into human life. Jesus, in whom the whole power of the divine Spirit has been focused, had died and risen from the dead in the mightiest of all the Spirit's mighty acts; and now, upon the Church that called Him Lord, there burst the mighty rushing wind of Pentecost."[11]

So we need to stop fighting it. Stop pushing. Stop going in the wrong direction, and follow! We do not need to know what God has in store for each of us or what he may require us to do. We only need to believe that through the Christ of Pentecost marvelous opportunities are there when we allow the Holy Spirit to have his way and listen to the wind!

A gentle breeze blows brushing our hair from our face.
We take no notice of it.
It is the way of the gentleness of God.
Always near, too often ignored.
The winds become stronger, clearing the yard of leaves,
    paper debris.
Our God is always ready to wash away all our un-
    cleanliness.
We ignore Him.
The winds become violent; seamen lower their sails.
Small boats head for shore.
Trees are blown down.
People become frightened and call upon their Lord for
    protection.
Why cannot we realize God can calm the winds as
    Jesus did?

Why won't we as a people recognize how great thou
   art?
The same God who is so gentle, kind and loving is with
   us always.
He will never leave nor forsake us.
Why not believe in Him?

MAUDE MAYES[12]

*Prayer: O wind of God, enter our hearts daily that we may be willing
to bring hope and courage to those who have become weighted down
with the burden of daily living. Help us to become a blessing to
others through the gentle wind of our spirit. Amen.*

MISSION SUNDAY

The mission of the church is not a matter of emphasis on one day or one season of the year but rather a mission that permeates the entire program of the church. Particular aspects of this mission are emphasized by churches throughout the year as a time to present the need and achievements of the mission program at home and overseas.

Outside the Pew

A young man stood just outside the back entrance of the church, talking on his cell phone. A backpack was on the ground beside him. I saw him as I pulled into the parking garage. I have to admit that I hoped he would move further down the alley before I was ready to leave the garage. After all, with the warnings and alerts being sounded these days, it is hard not to let the fear of the unknown cause anxiety. When I prepared to leave, he was still there talking on his phone. My first reaction was to wait or go in the other direction. After all, this was a downtown inner-city church. The doors were always locked. I would have to ring the bell to gain entrance to the building.

I hesitated for a moment and thought to myself, "O, you of little faith. You are on your way to Bible study, and you are already prejudging that young man. He is someone's son, husband, father, or brother. You are on your way to Bible study, and here you are hesitating." As I crossed the alley and approached the door, I smiled and said, "Good morning."

He moved the phone away from his ear and responded in this nice gentle voice: "Good morning to you, also, dear lady. I hope your day will be a good one."

"And yours also," I replied.

The buzzer sounded, and I went inside where it was safe.

My neighbor belongs to the Women's Fellowship of a local church, who spent the day as the guests of the Salvation Army. Following a period of fellowship and overall orientation, they traveled in vans to visit the Boys and Girls Club, the Alcohol and Drug Rehabilitation Center, and the halfway house for abused women. The trip took them through the "Samarias" of the city—the slum area housing projects, the boarded-up shops and houses, and the throngs of children playing in the streets while their mothers chatted with one another over decaying fences that separated one house from another.

As they rode along the narrow and less tended streets from one project to another, my neighbor overheard the person sitting behind her remark to her friend, "Why couldn't they have taken us over the interstate route instead of through this horrible area?" Her companion replied, "Maybe there are others like me who need to be reminded every once in a while of how the other half lives. I guess there is always a little more we can do."

Many of us may feel like the woman who preferred the interstate highway. After all, we have been bombarded with instant pictures of the devastation caused by war, natural disasters, ethnic cleansing, and starvation. During my private prayer time in Sunday morning worship, I recalled my experience on the way to Bible study and my neighbor's experience on the Salvation Army tour. Right then and there I decided that I needed a slogan for myself. I'd call it thinking "outside the pew." Perhaps we have been spending too much time "sitting in the pew" and not enough time "outside the pew," carrying out the mission of church.

I am reminded of a verbal exchange I overheard one Sunday morning. "A church school teacher asked a young boy in her class to give a definition of loving kindness. He replied, 'Now, let me think a minute.' Then he said, 'If I was hungry and you gave me a piece of bread, that would be kindness. If you were to put jelly on the bread, that would be loving kindness.'" I pray that God will give us hearts, moved by compassion toward the weak and the oppressed. Give us hearts ready and willing to provide loving kindness. Bread, and especially bread with jelly, would be a special treat for many.

We need to keep fresh in our memories the story in the gospel of Matthew about the five loaves and two fish:

> When it was evening, the disciples came to him and said, "This is a lonely place, and the day is over; send the crowds away to go into the villages and buy food for themselves." Jesus said, "They need not go away; you give them something to eat." They said to him, "We have only five loaves and two fish." And he said, "Bring them here to me." Then he ordered the crowds to sit down on the grass; and taking the five loaves and the two fish he looked up to heaven, and blessed, and broke and gave the loaves to the disciples, and the disciples gave them to the crowds. And they all ate and were satisfied. And they took up twelve baskets full of the broken pieces left over. (Mt. 14:15–20)

Kindness shown to someone should be the same whether we are inside or outside the pew! In Fanny J. Crosby's hymn "Rescue the Perishing" are these words:

> Touched by a loving heart,
> Wakened by kindness,
> Chords that were broken
> Will vibrate once more.

Prayer: Loving Lord, give us hearts moved by compassion toward the weary and the oppressed. When we can't invite them in to sit with us in the pew, help us to move outside to be with them. Equip us that we might be the channels through which your love may reach the hearts and lives of those who need to know and understand that someone cares. In your name we pray. Amen.

RECONCILIATION SUNDAY

Reconciliation is a special mission of the Christian Church (Disciples of Christ) for the elimination of the primary causes of racism in North America. The denomination has a history dating from the 1960s of sharing resources to address the racism of our society and the racism within the church. Other denominations and faith groups have similar observances. Reconciliation Sunday is held in the fall and provides an opportunity to think about what the church and individuals can do to alleviate the root causes of racism. An offering is received and used throughout the year.

How Do We Make Things Right?

Reconciliation is a good biblical word and, stated very simply, means, "making things right." How do we make things right?

One of my most memorable experiences of worship took place in a downtown church in San Francisco. The church was overflowing that Sunday morning, as it is every Sunday, with blacks and whites, young and old, hippies and straights, the haves and the have-nots, all sitting side by side. It was a cold, damp morning. As I sat waiting for the service to begin, I remember thinking how glad I was for the weather that caused me to wear my raincoat over my "dressy Sunday suit." I didn't look as conspicuous in my raincoat. After the service had begun, a poorly dressed and unkempt gentleman took the seat beside me. As the sermon was delivered, he appeared grateful for the warmth and comfort of the sanctuary as he nodded off every now and then.

When the minister completed his message, everyone stood and began singing the closing hymn, "We Shall Overcome." On the second verse, beginning with, "The Lord will see us through," the congregation began to join hands. As I sang I wanted to take the hand of the man beside me. But before I could muster up the courage, he reached out with a smile on his face and took mine. I learned that the service closed in this manner each Sunday as the sanctuary filled with joy and praise. I walked back to my hotel knowing that God's reconciling love had surely been in that place. You could feel God's presence there.

In contrast is something a friend once told me during a phone conversation. She had called me, needing someone to listen. She had been carrying some deep hurts and sorrows for a long time; it was even affecting her health. She told me: "You know, there is a big difference between scars and bruises; bruises heal, but scars are deep and always there."

Bitterness and unresolved disagreements can turn bruises into internal scars. What would happen if we put ourselves in the other person's place? What would happen if we could feel the hurt and experience the suppressed anger of those who have never known a fair chance in the mainstream of society? At times we are guilty of possessing an unforgiving spirit while having a long memory of our own slights and hurts.

Much reconciling needs to take place. Somehow we must find a way to acknowledge that the most segregated hour in many parts of the world is still the Sunday morning worship hour. How would you describe "reconciliation"? I describe it as forgiving, sharing, witnessing, communicating, loving my neighbor, and praying for those who feel alienated and alone. There is still much to "overcome."

> The rich and the poor meet together;
> the LORD is the maker of them all. (Prov. 22:2)

Prayer: We pray, O Lord, for those who feel alienated and alone. When we are wrong, may we be willing to admit it. When we are right, may we be a little easier to live and work with. Amen.

WORLD COMMUNION SUNDAY _____

The first Sunday in October is World Communion Sunday. Since 1940, this celebration at the table has expressed worldwide solidarity with Christians and serves as a sign of hope for the oneness to which we are called. Dr. Jesse M. Bader, a Christian Church (Disciples of Christ) minister, prompted by a development in the Presbyterian Church, proposed that, since communion is held in common by Christians everywhere, perhaps, on a particular day, all Christians could meet at the communion table and establish a new feeling of world community. He believed that this bridge of communion could be used to span the globe with the idea of world unity and peace.

Be Known to Us in Breaking Bread

One Sunday morning, just as the worship service began, a young man entered the sanctuary of a church located in the inner city. He edged his way slowly down the aisle to a vacant pew. As the service began and the congregation stood to sing the opening hymn, he moved a little closer to the front. He remained there until the minister began his message. Then he rose from the pew and nervously proceeded to a seat in the third row. Perhaps the minister's voice beckoned him to come closer. Several members became annoyed at what they perceived as his rudeness, but no one made a move to provide assistance.

As the time approached for the observance of holy communion, a young woman who was seated with her husband and young son moved forward and took a seat beside him. They shared the Lord's supper together as she helped him locate the bread and cup as the trays were passed. Following worship, a member approached the young woman wanting to know what had prompted her to leave her family to help the visitor. Without hesitation she replied, "It was obvious he was blind and wanted to be nearer to the front of the sanctuary. Was I the only one who saw him using his white cane? How could I just sit and not welcome him to the "Table"?

When Helen Keller was asked whether or not living blind was the worst affliction in the world, she is said to have replied: "No, I think the worst thing in the world is to have eyes to see and not see. There is no lovelier way to thank God for your sight than by giving a helping hand to someone in the dark."

Today on this World Communion Sunday Christians have gathered, or will gather, about his table spread with the sacred emblems. There may be a difference in the meeting place, order of worship, and type of emblems provided; but everywhere those who gather will be bound to Christ and to one another by the strong bonds of love and fellowship. They will feel and experience the oneness and unity about the one table.

Some will gather in small churches or stately cathedrals; others in military chapels, on shipboard, or on the battlefield. Members of the clergy or designated elders will bring the sacred emblems to those who live alone in private residences or those confined to hospitals, nursing facilities, or assisted living and retirement centers.

Let us consider how Rosa Page Welch, a twentieth-century African American Disciples singer, described communion: "The miracle of Communion means the rich bowing down with the poor, the learned with the unlearned, the clean with the filthy, the master with the slave, the privileged with the deprived, the white with the black, the black with the white,"[13] *and,* I would add, "peoples of all races and cultures, including those who are blind."

In memory of the Savior's love,
we keep the sacred feast,
where every humble, contrite heart
is made a welcome guest.[14]

THOMAS COTTERILL

Prayer: Gracious God, with humble gratitude we accept your loving invitation to share in the joyous celebration that you have prepared for us. We thank you for the length of your table around which we all may gather. Amen.

CHILDREN'S EMPHASIS _____

The observance placing emphasis on the work with children in the Christian Church (Disciples of Christ) began in 1880 with an emphasis on world missions. Years later, the first Sunday in June was established as Children's Day, a time for presentations with an emphasis on the needs of children and appeals to support world missions. Later it became a part of Christian Family Week. Today Disciples participate in Light a Candle for Children and the Observance of National Children's Sabbath, which is supported by more than 150 denominations and religious groups. Christians are invited to make a personal commitment to ongoing prayer and action on behalf of children—all children, those within our churches and those beyond our doorsteps. The emphasis is still on missions!

Listen to the Children

At the close of an interesting school day the children in the first grade classroom were lining up to walk to the school bus. As the substitute teacher, I was very anxious that the children not be late. One little bright-eyed, freckled-face girl didn't get in line. She walked over, grabbed my sleeve, and blurted out, "I sure do like you. Do you know why? Because even when you're fussing, you look like you're smiling!"

Years later, one Sunday morning the director of Christian education asked if I would help with the nursery/kindergarten class. The person who was supposed to assist the teacher hadn't arrived, but a lot of kids had. I always like a challenge, especially when it involves children, so I agreed to help. It had been a while since I had been in a classroom situation with very young children, but I knew it would be fun. The boys and girls were gathering on the designated rug in front of the teacher. The little girls were up front, and four boys were sitting or lying as far back as they could without being on the bare floor.

I went in, said hello, and took a seat in one of those tiny kindergarten chairs. The class began with the singing of fun songs. Then the teacher guided the children in prayer and began the lesson. The little girls sat and listened; the boys continued "their game" of pulling a leg or trying to pull off a shoe. The teacher did all she could to capture their attention, but it wasn't to be. I knew I had to do something. I slid off my chair onto the rug and moved over so I could sit near the boys. They were amused by my action and calmed down a little. Every once in a while I had to reach out and gently grab a foot or a leg. The teacher didn't skip a beat. After all, she had the attention of the girls. Soon I noticed one of the boys (whose name I would later discover was Grant) edging closer and closer to me. When he was beside me, I put my arm around him and smiled. He laid his head in my lap and began rubbing my arm and patting my cheek. As he looked up at me, he whispered: "I love you."

I whispered back that I loved him, too.

Then he asked: "Do you know why I love you?"

"No," I said.

"Because you remind me of my grandmother."

When the church service was over, the teacher took me to meet Grant's mother. We chatted, and I told her how much I enjoyed being with her son and how moved I was by the comments he had made. With tears in her eyes, she told me that his only grandmother had died a month earlier and he missed her so much. Every Sunday since that day, Grant and I share hugs, sometimes a kiss, and have become best friends.

Our religious faith is one that challenges the ordinary human standards by holding that the ideal spirit is that of a child. "Unless you turn and become like children, you will never enter the kingdom of heaven" (Mt. 18:3). Our culture tends to glorify adulthood and wisdom and worldly prudence, but the gospel reverses all this. The gospel says, in effect, that we must become tender and full of wonder and unspoiled by the hard skepticism on which we often pride ourselves.

Remember that a smile or a hug costs us nothing, but it gives much. It can enrich the lives of those who receive it without making poorer those who give it. It takes but a moment, but the memory of it sometimes lasts forever. It cannot be bought and is of no value to anyone until it is given away. When you are tired and have had a hard day, try to look like you're smiling. Remember that no one needs a smile or a hug more than a child and persons who have none to give.

Prayer: O Lord, lover of all children everywhere, you were never too busy to listen and give them guidance. May the example of your love create within each of us a new attitude and compassion for those who suffer this day because of our lack of patience and understanding. Guide our thoughts and hearts that we may at least be willing to share a smile, a hug, and a portion of our resources with "the least of these." Amen.

NATIONAL BIBLE SUNDAY

The American Bible Society was established by the churches of the United States in 1816 and advocated a special Bible Day as early as 1900. Bible Sunday was first celebrated on Sunday, December 5, 1915, and continues to the present day. National Bible Sunday , previously known as Universal Bible Sunday, is generally observed on the third Sunday in November but can be celebrated on any Sunday during the year.

Enemy-forgiving Love

The late Dr. Dwight E. Stevenson told a fascinating and almost forgotten true story:

> Following World War II, Japanese soldiers on the island of Panay in the Philippines massacred eleven American Baptist missionaries. One couple requested and got a half-hour's reprieve for private prayer. Then they were killed. Their daughter in the States, when she learned of the massacre, was consumed with bitterness. Then she wondered what her Mother and Father had prayed about during that last half hour. Without question she knew they had prayed that the Japanese soldiers be forgiven. She went to the nearest prisoner of war camp where she gave herself in volunteer service to the Japanese prisoners. She did it with complete forgiveness. The prisoners responded to her kindness with increasing curiosity. Finally one spoke up, "Why do you do this?" She told them, but they could not understand such enemy-forgiving love.
>
> At Osaka there lived a farmer, the disillusioned Mitsuo Fuchida, former captain of the Japanese navy. He had led the 359 planes that had bombed

Pearl Harbor. A shipload of prisoners came back to Japan, repatriated at the close of the war; and Captain Fuchida went to meet the ship. One of the prisoners, Uraga, told the mystifying story of the American girl who had served them in the prison camp. Fuchida could not understand such enemy-forgiving love.

Shortly Fuchida was summoned to Tokyo to appear before General MacArthur. He emerged into Tokyo through the Sheybuya Railway Station. He was handed a gospel tract which told of an American bombardier who had been taken prisoner by the Japanese and who had recovered his Christian perspective in prison by reading the Bible. When the war was over, he had returned to Japan to serve his former enemies as a missionary. After reading the tract, Fuchida went to a book-store and bought a copy of the New Testament. He read the Gospel of Luke until he came to the crucifixion and Jesus' words, "Father, forgive them for they know not what they do." Then he knew the secret of enemy-forgiving love! There on the streets of Tokyo near him stood a sound wagon. He strode to it, requested the use of the microphone, and to the startled passersby, made this announcement: "This is Captain Mitsuo Fuchida. I led the attack of Pearl Harbor. I want to tell you that I have become a Christian.[15]

Dr. Stevenson wrote that Fuchida met God in Christ though the human community of faith and love where sin and forgiveness are real and then came to know him by name through the living Bible.

Hundreds of Vietnamese refugees found safe haven on the island of Pulau Bidong located off the coast of Malaysia. Worship services were provided once a week on "Religion Hill" for members of the newly formed Protestant church. (See "Let Every Heart Prepare Him Room" on page 2). During my visit we shared refreshments, sang Christmas carols, and enjoyed a time of sharing. Those present were very anxious to learn about America and especially what the church was doing for the refugees who had been resettled there. One of the young women asked a question in Vietnamese, and Commandant Tommy translated. "She wants to know what the churches in the United States do to help the refugees learn more about Christianity. Are they given Bibles?" he asked for her.

Sometimes I am prone to speak and then think. I proceeded to tell them that there was a group in the United States called the "Gideons" who provided the sponsors with Bibles in Vietnamese and English. These were then shared with the new arrivals at the appropriate time. As soon as the words were out of my mouth, I thought to myself, "Why did you tell them that? They have no way of knowing about the Gideons." Then Commandant Tommy, before translating what I had said, leaned over from the bench on which he was seated, looked at me and said, "Rev. Dorothy, I am a Gideon. I first became a Christian when a stranger gave me a Gideon Bible while I was stationed in the Philippines."

For once in my life I was glad I had spoken before I thought. After all, this was the man who was instrumental in building the places of worship on Religion Hill. He said that the refugees, who had lost everything, needed at least one thing to hold on to—their faith in a God.

It is impossible to know how many individuals throughout the world have come to Christ because someone gave them a Bible. Often the Bibles in our homes sit on the coffee table or nightstand and go unopened until there is a crisis. National Bible Sunday is a good time to brush them off and, as Dr. Stevenson suggests, "come face to face with Jesus."

"The truths of the Bible are not pebbles to be picked up as we saunter along the beach. They are nuggets of gold to be mined out of hard rock by the sweat of our brow, and they are precious beyond price."[16]

Prayer: Dear loving and caring Savior, your word continues to be "a lamp unto our feet and a light unto our path." Help us to grow in understanding and knowledge that we may also grow in our desire to share the Bible with others. We ask that you continue to bless those who translate, distribute and teach your Word throughout the world. Amen.

Meditations
for the
Civil Year

New Year's Sunday _____

New Year's Sunday is observed on the Sunday preceding January 1. The day provides an opportunity for an appraisal of the past and the challenge of the future for the individual and the church. During the time of the Julian calendar the year began on March 25. With the introduction of the Gregorian calendar in the sixteenth century, New Year's Day was changed to January 1.

God Is a Surprise

Most of any day's delights and highlights are found in its surprises—a glimpse of beauty in new fallen snow, the sight of a rainbow as you round the bend in the road, the moon appearing in the darkened sky as you walk to your car after a meal with friends.

Usually I go through the garage and down the driveway to get the morning paper. But on this day, for some reason, I decided to use the front door. As I stepped down the second step to the sidewalk, I noticed a huge spider hanging in a shrub by one silken thread. I paused a moment and looked at him. I knew he was out of my reach without a ladder so I silently said, "I'll get you later," and continued to the mailbox. I forgot all about my "unwanted friend" as I became absorbed in the day's activities.

Several days later I took my little dog, Sprocket, with me to get the morning paper. Again I used the front door. As we passed by the shrub, I noticed the spider was not where he had been when I first saw him. I backed up a step and took a second look. What a surprise! The sun's rays spotlighted this huge glistening web connecting the shrub to one side of the window. The spider sat in the middle of his woven creation enjoying the sunlight. He seemed to be saying to me: "Here I am! See what I've created for you. Come get me, but remember if you destroy me, you destroy my beautiful creation as well." Perhaps you've already made your New Year's resolutions or decided you are not going to make them this year. Some of us look to the New Year as a time to get things in order so that we can go about our days with more structure. That seems strange to me. If we think about it, most of any day's delights are in its surprises.

We know from experience that our greatest delights come from the unexpected glimpse of a robin perched just outside our window reminding us that spring is on its way, the chance meeting with a friend from years gone by, the insightful or funny comment of one of our children or grandchildren after making a discovery, or an unexpected job promotion that makes a day memorable.

Yet we keep arranging and rearranging, sometimes even avoiding strangers or new neighbors, as if we wanted to insulate ourselves completely against surprises. Some work harder at it than others. We establish routes and routines and patterns and become upset if they're broken. But others know the joy and significance of surprises. They will, more often than not, take a new turn in the road to see what lies over the brow of a hill. They will try a new venture in life to see what bright things might be learned from it. Much can be said for the familiar and the orderly, but surprises help keep our spirits young.

This year let us each make a resolution not to make a resolution but to wait and look for God's inexplicable surprises, the surprises that cannot be explained. Let us take the time to open our eyes and discover the beauty in simple things that are near at hand. God just might weave a new pattern, a new thing, using each one of us.

Restless Weaver, still conceiving new life—
now and yet to be—
binding all your vast creation
in one living tapestry:
you have called us to be weavers.
Let your love guide all we do.

With your Reign of Peace our pattern,
We will weave your world anew.

O. I. CRICKET HARRISON[1]

Prayer: Great and marvelous are your works, O Lord. Help us to enter this New Year on tiptoe, anticipating with joy and eyes wide open the new things you will reveal to us. Guide us that we may confront the future with quiet minds and resourceful hearts, knowing that even during uncertain times we may receive and know the joy and significance of surprises. Amen.

FREEDOM AND DEMOCRACY SUNDAY_____
(INDEPENDENCE SUNDAY)

This day is observed on the Sunday preceding July 4, which marks the anniversary of the signing of the Declaration of Independence in 1776. The American colonists who proclaimed their independence were affirming their inherent rights as persons. Following the signing of the Declaration, John Adams is reported to have written his wife: "It ought to be commemorated as the day of deliverance by solemn acts of devotion to Almighty God."

Freedom Isn't Free

In the late 1960s and early 1970s, a group of high school students formed a choral group that was a local affiliate of the national group "Up with People." The teenagers in this small town wanted to tell through song what was right with America and to share with others some of the positive things youth were doing. They carried their message to events throughout the area.

Following the introduction and statement of purpose, their program began with a fast-paced rendition of "Freedom Isn't Free." With all the harmony and volume they could muster they sang: "Freedom isn't free. Freedom isn't free. You have to pay the price. You have to sacrifice for your liberty."[2]

What is freedom? Is it free? Someone has aptly said that freedom does not mean individuals can do as they please. It means that they are given an opportunity to work toward becoming what they wish to be. I remember one year when, on the first day back after the July 4th holiday, my coworkers and I were enjoying lunch and discussing the day with a young Vietnamese interpreter. When one of us asked Hong what he had done, he replied: "We watched the celebrations on television. I told my Mother: 'Hey. This is our country. We're Americans now.' So I stood and put my hand over my heart as the Star Spangled Banner was sung. Did you do that too?" he asked. Before anyone could answer, he said: "For the first time I realized we were free."

We shared our activities, but they seemed so trivial and shallow. One had gone shopping; another had enjoyed a picnic with some friends. Two had cleaned house, and one had worked in the yard. We had to admit, at least to ourselves, that none of us had stood in reverence as the national anthem was sung. Perhaps we felt so secure that we took our freedom for granted.

We like to think of freedom as being able to do whatever we please as long as we don't break the law. Dr. Leslie D. Weatherhead wrote, "The only way to enjoy freedom is to voluntarily accept bondage." Simon Peter reminded us that the Christian is free, proclaiming that he was a slave to Christ. Seems rather foolish, doesn't it? Free but in bondage; free but a slave.

One afternoon I noticed several neighbor boys playing paddleball. I watched as each tried to hit the captive rubber ball attached to his particular paddle by a piece of rubber string. After a while it appeared that they had gone beyond the desire to hit the balls; the goal now was to see who could hit his the hardest. All went well until one of the balls broke away and landed in a neighbor's yard. They were free to hit the ball because it was bound to the paddle; it was in bondage. When the elastic broke, the ball could no longer be hit with that same freedom.

The key to freedom and strength has meaning because we are bound. "For you were called to freedom, brethren; only do not use your freedom as an opportunity for the flesh, but through love be servants of one another" (Gal. 5:13).

Prayer: Almighty God, we express our gratitude for our freedom, especially the freedom to worship you. We ask forgiveness when we take it for granted and fail to follow your teachings. Help us to realize that we live in an interdependent world. We pray that the America we hold so dear will continue to be a blessing and haven of rest for those whose freedom has not yet been secured. Grant that our desires will always be in accordance with your will. Amen.

LABOR SUNDAY

Labor Sunday has been observed on the day before Labor Day since 1910. The first Labor Day was celebrated in New York in 1882 on the suggestion of Peter J. McGuire, founder of the United Brotherhood of Carpenters. Mr. McGuire suggested that the first Monday in September be the day because it was about halfway between Independence Day and Thanksgiving. In 1894 Congress passed a law making legal the observance of Labor Day as a public holiday.

God Is No Gentleman

Poet Carl Sandburg captures an active God getting up and putting on overalls to go to work everyday in his poem "God Is No Gentleman."

In the creation story one refrain answers each act of creation: "and God saw that it was good."

When a group of "seniors" get together, the conversation often turns to the subject of having too much or not enough to do. The feeling seems to be that "our productive days are over." Then the conversation quickly moves to the topic of downsizing—the getting rid of those years of clutter.

I have been trying to downsize by disposing of the hundreds of books that my late husband and I obtained over the years. Sometimes the day's work evolved around seeing how many shelves could be cleared in a week. But there was a problem. I'd remove books from the shelf, put them in a box, and then in a day or two I'd go through the box and put many of them back on the shelf. Some had been too much a part of our lives to let them go. Just by looking at the titles, a stranger could determine the type of employment we had enjoyed.

On this Labor Day Sunday many continue to be a part of the work force, while others feel isolated. As individuals grow older, their ability to be gainfully employed may cease, but the cycle of life and work ebbs and flows. God continues to run the universe.

One proud grandmother recently shared the good news that her grandson Emerson had obtained his first summer job as a "paper boy." Other youth begin their journey of employment by taking out the trash, mowing the lawn, doing laundry, or washing the dishes. Charles Kinsley gave us words of wisdom when he said: "Thank God every morning when you wake up that you have something to do which must be done, whether you like it or not. Being forced to work and forced to do your best will breed in you a hundred virtues which the idle never know."[3]

What each of us does as individuals is important, for we are exchanging a day of our life for it. When tomorrow comes, this day will be gone forever, leaving in its place something we traded for it. Each of us in our individual work, whatever it may be, also contributes to the life of others. While we are making our contributions, others are contributing as well. They collect the trash; pave the roads; or keep the electricity, gas, telephones, computers, or televisions going. There are doctors and nurses, policemen and firemen, rescue and utility workers, airline pilots and truck drivers, farmers and dairymen all going about their work, often unseen and at all hours of the day and night.

God is calling us to put on our overalls and join with him as we labor and work for a better tomorrow.

And God will see that it is good.

Let us, then, be up and doing,
    With a heart for any fate;
Still achieving, still pursuing,
    Learn to labor and to wait.

HENRY WADSWORTH LONGFELLOW[4]

Prayer: We offer our prayers, O Lord, in gratitude for all those who have to work today to maintain the essential services on which we depend. Grant us renewed strength for tomorrow's day of work. Amen.

THANKSGIVING SUNDAY _____

Governor William Bradford of the Plymouth Colony instituted Thanksgiving Day in 1621. Around 1630 it became an annual observance after each harvest. Other colonies soon took up the practice. President George Washington recommended in 1789 and 1795 that all set apart and observe a day of public thanksgiving. In 1863 Abraham Lincoln issued a proclamation calling upon the nation to set apart the last Thursday in November as a day of Thanksgiving. In Canada, English explorer Martin Frobisher held a formal Thanksgiving ceremony in 1578, but the present celebration in October was established by the Canadian Parliament in 1957.[5] Thanksgiving is a distinctly North American holiday. Thanksgiving Sunday is celebrated on the Sunday preceding Thanksgiving Day.

Give Thanks in All Circumstances

Who would dream that a flat tire and monsoon rains would combine to be a blessing and cause one to give thanks? The rented station wagon that was taking us on our journey 150 miles up-country from Monrovia, Liberia, was certainly not new, and the tires were nearly bald. But who is concerned about such things when there is so much to see? We passed the worker's huts, the American style ranch houses at Firestone Rubber Plantation, and the zoo where the keeper coaxed an elephant to the fence by shaking a large box of cornflakes. We glimpsed coffee trees, orange and pineapple trees, and goats roaming free along the side of the road.

Then the rain came, along with the flat tire! The driver suggested that perhaps it would be best if we did not put on our plastic raincoats; the heat and humidity were very high. We proceeded to do so anyway. After all, what did he know about such things? Or so we thought. We soon regretted that decision and wished we had followed his advice as we walked the short distance up the dirt road to a small village. We quickly shed the raincoats in the hope of drying out as we took shelter under our "coffee tree umbrella."

A kind woman who spoke excellent English came to greet us, offering us shelter under the slanting thatched roof of her home. We marveled at the beauty of the cannas growing in the yard of this humble dwelling. After the rain had subsided, she picked some green coffee beans from the tree under which we first sought shelter and suggested that we take them home to remind us of our visit. All too quickly, it seemed, the tire was changed, the rains had ceased, and we said good-bye to our new friend. The discomfort and the inconvenience of the flat tire and the rain had turned into a blessing. The hospitality of our hostess had touched our hearts forever.

Few countries in the world have been able year after year to celebrate a day of thanks under such consistently prosperous conditions as we here in North America. Yet that very prosperity sometimes obscures the real nature and secret of living a thankful life. More and more we have become associated with material abundance. We take pride in the physical strength drawn from fertile fields, rich mines, and thriving commercial centers. All too often we give thanks for those things. Sometimes we need to be reminded that our forefathers were thankful before they were prosperous. The lesson we received from them is that the spirit that made this country great was one that enabled the people to give thanks even in times of adversity.

For what will we give thanks this year? Will it be for the kindness of an elderly neighbor who took in our mail while we were away, the assistance given by a stranger when our car broke down, the doctors and nurses who cared for us when we were ill, the truck driver who continued driving through the stormy night to make sure his cargo arrived at the grocery store in time for the Thanksgiving festivities?

Each year I continue to give thanks for the friendship of that gracious individual who welcomed strangers from a foreign land and shared the shelter of her home.

Prayer: *O God, whatever the circumstances, may we give thanks not only this day but every day throughout the year. Save us from being so focused on our own problems that the needs of others escape us. Amen.*

Meditations
for
Days In-Between

Living with Mirrors and Windows

Glass is one of the oldest inventions. Its manufacture was an established industry in Egypt more than 3,500 years ago. It has countless applications—light bulbs, dishes for eating and drinking, reflectors, and beads to name a few. And don't forget mirrors and windows.

The mirror is one of the weirdest of manmade items. It is made of a pane of glass coated on the back with silver so that light cannot pass through. The light is reflected, allowing us to see an image of ourselves. A mirror does not open to the other side of the wall but to our own side. The image we see is of ourselves. We often reflect upon that reflection.

A story is told of the mythological character, Narcissus, who wasted away because he fell in love with his own facial features, and could pull himself away from his reflection in the water, not even to eat. All of us resemble Narcissus to the extent that we are fascinated by our physical appearance. While standing in front of this object we call a mirror, we not only observe the contours of our physique but also engage in such daily rituals as applying make-up, combing our hair, putting on jewelry, shaving, and straightening ties. Sometimes we may not enjoy the reflected image. The mirror may reveal unwanted wrinkles, graying hair, and extra inches around the waist. Nevertheless, we are almost magnetically pulled to spend a portion of our time gazing into a mirror.

A window is different. At first it was merely an opening to provide light and air in a building. Buildings or factories were designed so that windows could be placed in appropriate areas to let in the maximum amount of light. Windows were first made of clear glass. Later, some were made of tinted glass or even painted to keep out the glare. As churches were able to afford them, stained-glass windows were installed to use the light to create a beautiful panorama of colored pictures to help tell the story of religious faith.

Much of the life we lead is determined by what we think of that inverted image we see in the mirror, our approval of it or our disapproval. A woman was admiring a painting framed under glass in an art gallery. Suddenly, the sun filled the room with light. Its rays caused the woman to see her own image in the glass. She immediately opened her purse, took out her comb, and began to tidy up her hair. She did not see the beauty of the painting because the image of herself was in the way. Her need to satisfy herself kept her from seeing the beauty the artist created.

We spend time and resources getting face-lifts and tummy tucks, applying wrinkle cream, and visiting tanning salons, all to make us appear different. We depend on the mirror because it is the only clue we have to the way others might view us. Sometimes we become so conscious of our own image that we miss the beauty around us and within us.

What if we exchanged the mirror for a window through which we could rediscover a Savior who allows us to be who we are: loving, caring followers of the way? Suppose we removed the silver from the mirrors that permit us only to see our own need, and instead peered through the windows to enjoy a brand new world filled with the beauty of God's creation. Mirrors and windows are both important tools that, when used properly, bring us into the very presence of God.

> Finally, brethren, whatever is true, whatever is honorable, whatever is just, whatever is pure, whatever is lovely, whatever is gracious, if there is any excellence, if here is anything worthy of praise, think about these things. What you have learned and received and heard and seen in me, do; and the God of peace will be with you. (Phil. 4:8, 9)

Prayer: Come, Lord Jesus, and be with us that we may have the courage to look into the mirror of our lives and strip away those things that keep us from attending to the business of your church. Save us from being so enamored with our own problems that the needs of your other children escape us. Amen.

He Went to a Lonely Place

Have you ever wondered where Jesus got his strength for the strenuous days, where he got the understanding and sympathy for others, or how he could speak with so much authority? Perhaps it was because, "After he had dismissed the crowd, he went up on the mountain by himself to pray" (Mt. 14:23).

We each need a place to be alone, a place to pray. One Sunday morning following worship I was greeting those in attendance when a young boy came through the line with his parents. As I leaned down to take his hand, he looked up at me and whispered, "I have a lonely place where I go to think." Then he told me about his special place. A creek ran behind his house. Nearby stood a large tree. When he needed time to himself or to think through something that was bothering him, he would go and sit under the tree to think and pray. He shared his secret place with me because I had chosen as the focal point of my message Mark 1:35, "And in the morning, a great while before day, he rose and went out to a lonely place, and there he prayed."

One of the hardest things for many of us to do is to sit and be still. Our bodies and minds are so programmed for going and doing, for staying busy. We can't get our body and mind to slow down, much less relax. Following heart bypass surgery my cardiologist insisted that one of the things I had to do when I went home was to have bed rest for at least an hour each afternoon. I didn't have to sleep. I just had to "lay still" for an hour! Then he said, "I know this will be hard for you to do. I guess we'll have to 'Velcro' you to the bed to keep you there."

Over the years I've learned that nothing can restore an anxious, healing heart or a troubled mind like quiet time spent in a lonely place. Being still is hard, but sometimes the hardest part is finding a place in the midst of all the noise and busyness of the day where we can be still. We don't always have access to a large tree beside the creek.

An old German proverb says, "When in prayer you clasp your hands, God opens his." God will open his hand to us even if our lonely place is waiting in the dentist office, stuck in rush-hour traffic, waiting for a child's ball game to end, or waiting for the water to boil as we prepare our breakfast.

The chief ingredient in prayer is always a sensitive and responsive heart. Perhaps we need to learn to look within no matter where we are. There we will find our lonely place, and God will meet us there.

God answers prayer, sometime when hearts are weak,
He gives the very gifts believers seek.
But often faith must learn a deeper rest,
And trust God's silence when he does not speak.
For he whose name is Love will send the best.
Stars may burn out, nor mountain walls endure,
But God is true, his promises are sure
For those who seek.

MYRA GOODWIN PLANTZ[1]

Women, Wells, and Water Jars

When I was in the Middle East, one of the places I wanted to visit was the well where Jesus met the Samaritan woman. In the evening after our group had visited the site, my traveling companion and I sat on the balcony of the Y.M.C.A. and looked out over the old walled city of Jerusalem as we discussed the events of the day. We turned to John 4 to read the story of Jesus and the woman at the well.

We came to the twenty-seventh verse, which tells of the disciples returning and finding Jesus talking to a woman. "So the woman left her water jar, and went away into the city, and said to the people, 'Come, see a man who told me all that I ever did. Can this be the Christ?'" (Jn. 4:28–29)

She left her water jar!

This Samaritan woman was so sure that Jesus was who he said he was and became so excited that she left her water jar and ran into town and "panted" out her story. This lonesome, passionate woman became a persuasive evangelist and the first to convey Christ's mission beyond the bounds of his Jewish homeland.

What about us? Would we leave our most priceless possessions—our water jars, whatever they may be—and go tell others about the one who offered "living water"?

Wells are the places where new things can happen, where fresh insights can be gained, where life-giving strength and sustaining power can be given to those who thirst. Water jars are those things in our lives that stand in our way. They are the things or issues that keep us from going forth and telling the good news to those who have not heard. Remember, the Samaritan woman became so excited that she left her most precious and needed possession behind.

What would happen if Christian women decided to rise up with one voice and declare, "There must be peace; it will begin with me here and now"?

And what would happen if we, you and I, were to leave our water jars and proclaim to all we meet: Come learn about this Prince of Peace who will provide the world with living water?

Whispers of Love

A few years ago I was serving as a supply pastor for a small congregation some seventy-five miles from home. This particular morning I was traveling down the interstate highway when I began thinking, almost out loud, to myself, "Why am I doing this? I have worked hard all week and feel tired and weary. I have so little time and energy to give these folks. What can I possibly do for them that someone else couldn't do equally as well?"

When I parked in front of the church a few minutes later, the usual greeters were there to welcome me and say how happy they were that I had taken the time to come. At eleven o'clock the service began, and the small group of God's faithful joined in singing: "Angels descending bring from above echoes of mercy, whispers of love."

This fascinating combination of words penned by Fanny J. Crosby in the hymn "Blessed Assurance" leaped out at me as they had never done before. I almost lost my place as I thought to myself: "That's it! That's what I can give: 'whispers of love.'" I don't have to perform great miracles or feel that I have to assist them in becoming what they aren't or what they can never be. All I am called to do is share with them and help them share whispers of love with others.

Love is the most universally desired quality in the world—the high and the low, the rich and the poor, the young and the old—all crave acts of love. It is also the most enduring thing in the world. Under pressure, tension, or suffering, it shines most brightly. It never fails. It endures. But whoever saw love? It is like the wind. It is felt. Its presence is recognized through things that are seen. It is a happening. It can become known through a friendly handshake, a warm embrace, or some deed of kindness.

Jesus gave repeated and surprising emphasis to what many have called obscure service—service with little or no fanfare. He spoke of the importance of the cup of cold water given in love. He insisted that to feed the hungry and visit the sick were of infinite value. We come in daily contact with persons who need our love, but we fail to act because we feel that what we have to offer is so small or insignificant compared to what someone else might provide. Let us never forget that a friendly word—a whisper of love—could cleanse the heart, banish doubt, or conquer fear.

Prayer: O Lord, teach us the worth of a small deed. Remind us how many there are who need a smile or a friendly hand. Help us to remember that often people need our love most when they are unlovable and filled with bitterness and anger. Use us as channels of your blessing through our whispers of love. Amen.

Special
Services

Blessing of the Hands Service for Elders

Setting

At the front of room place two small tables, each with a basin and a pitcher of water. Towels for drying the elder's hands will be needed and may be placed at a convenient location near the tables.

Participants Other than the Elders

Four persons will be needed (plus an organist or pianist and the choir, if they are invited to participate): two clergy or other designated individuals will wash and bless the hands, and two individuals will be responsible for drying the hands. The organist, pianist, and/or choir will accompany and provide appropriate music as the hands are washed.

The duties of each are as follows:

- The clergy will be responsible for pouring a small amount of water over the hands of each elder as he or she approaches the table and places his or her hands over the basin. The clergy will place one hand gently on the shoulder of the elder. Using the other hand, the clergy will pour a small amount of water over the hands, and offer the prayer of blessing as the water is being poured.

- The individuals who are standing to the side of the tables dry each person's hands and say, "Bless you." As the first two elders leave, two more approach the tables; and the ritual is repeated.

- The organist, pianist, and/or choir will accompany and lead in the singing of the hymns and provide other music where appropriate. Perhaps a solo or instrumental music may be provided as the elders come forward and participate in the blessing.

Clergy Prayer of Blessing

(Print the prayer on two cards. Place one on each table so that the clergy may refer to them as needed.)

God of life, Creator of the Universe, we humbly ask your blessing upon these human hands that you have created. May they be instruments of your peace. May they bring your comfort and compassion to each life that they touch. Amen.

The Order of Worship

Two orders of worship are provided. One is in outline form for the bulletin or program. The names of the participants will need to be added. The other includes the entire service with opening remarks, prayers, hymn suggestions, and meditations.

1. Bulletin

Front cover—Design of your choosing plus the following:

Blessing of the Hands
A Service of Dedication
for the Elders of (*church name*)
Place and Date

(Listing of the names of elders may be included on the inside front cover or on the back of the bulletin.)

Inside—Welcome and Opening Remarks
Opening Hymn—"Come, Holy Spirit, Fill This Place," verses 1, 2, and 4, *Chalice Hymnal,* no. 269
Invocation
Reading 1—Psalm 23
Reading 2—Take My Hands
Reflection—Using My Hands
Blessing of Hands
Closing Prayer

Closing Hymn—"He Touched Me," *Chalice Hymnal,* no. 564
Benediction
Reception to follow—location

2. Order of worship with prayers and meditations for Blessing of Hands

WELCOME AND LEADER'S OPENING REMARKS

We come together to participate in a simple ritual asking God to bless the work of our hands. We ask that in our touch, in our care for others, in whatever work our hands are called upon to perform, God's love and blessing will be communicated.

We will use water in our ritual and a simple prayer as we ask God's blessing upon each elder's hands as they come forward two by two a little later in the service.

Water is a powerful symbol in many faith traditions. Water is a reminder of the waters of baptism where one is called to live, love, and touch others in the way Jesus lived, loved, and touched throughout his life. We ask that our hands communicate God's love, as did the hands of Jesus.

OPENING HYMN

"Come, Holy Spirit, Fill This Place," verses 1, 2, 4, *Chalice Hymnal,* no. 269.

INVOCATION

Gracious and loving God, be with us as we gather to ask your blessing upon the work of the hands of the elders of (*name of your church*). We acknowledge you as the Creator of the universe. By your touch we are made whole. May the touch of our hands communicate your love, comfort, and hope through our service as elders. Amen.

READING 1: THE 23RD PSALM (TEV)

The LORD is my shepherd;
I have everything I need.

He lets me rest in fields of green grass
    and leads me to quiet pools of fresh water.
He gives me new strength.
He guides me in the right paths,
    as he has promised.
Even if I go through the deepest darkness,
    I will not be afraid, LORD,
    for you are with me.
Your shepherd's rod and staff protect me.
You prepare a banquet for me,
    where all my enemies can see me;
 you welcome me as an honored guest
    and fill my cup to the brim.
I know that your goodness and love will be with me all
    my life;
    and your house will be my home as long as I live.

READING 2: TAKE MY HANDS

Take my hands and make them as your own.
Use them for your kingdom here on earth.
Consecrate them to your care,
Anoint them for your service wherever
You may need your gospel to be sown.

Take my hands, they speak now for my heart,
And by their actions they will show their love.
Guard them on their daily course,
Be their strength and guiding force
To ever serve the Trinity above.

Take my hands, I give them now to you, Lord.
Prepare them for the service of your name.
Open them to human need and their love.
They'll sow your seed,
So all may know the love and hope you gave.
Take my hands, take my hands, O Lord.[1]

REFLECTION

Leader: Hands are wonderful symbols. Hands greet, shake, touch, operate, wave, and bless. They can slap, destroy, tear down, cause misery, but at the same time they can be used to build, help, console, and caress. The most important thing hands do is touch. They touch others and touch hearts.

They are a wonderful symbol and sign of God's love found approximately one thousand times in the scriptures. An interesting Hebrew expression translated "to consecrate" literally reads, "to fill the hand," meaning that without consecration we have little or nothing to offer to God. Our prayer now is that our hands might be the hands that God uses to comfort those who are sick, befriend those who are lonely, care for those who are faced with the death of a loved one or friend, and share and celebrate with friends in their times of joy.

BLESSING OF HANDS

Will all those leading in the service please take their places. The elders will now come forward two by two (one or two lines). You may return to your seats following the blessing.

CLOSING PRAYER

Our loving and merciful God, we come before you offering thanks for the gift of your love. We pray especially for the elders whose hands have been blessed. Give skill and tender care to those special hands, and kindness and sympathy to their hearts. Give to us all singleness of purpose and the strength to lift the burden of those we serve. May your love and comfort be communicated through the work of our hands. Amen.

CLOSING SONG

"He Touched Me," *Chalice Hymnal,* no. 564

Installation Services for Elders or Deacons

It is suggested that the elders be installed during the morning worship service or at a special dinner. The meditation may be given by the minister, board chair, outgoing chair of elders, or other appropriate person. The words of installation may be given by the same person or someone else chosen to share this honor.

Elders serving for the first time may be presented with a Chalice Lapel Pin or a book as a symbol of recognition. Pins are available from Cokesbury (1-800-672-1789), and books such as *Your Calling as an Elder* or *Your Calling as a Deacon* are available from Christian Board of Publication at 1-800-366-3383.

Service 1: God Does Not Call You to Be Perfect————

LEADER

Being asked to serve as an elder means that someone or a group of individuals noticed something special about each of you. As you begin this time of service, you are encouraged to cultivate that "something special" about yourself. It may be the ability to talk with others over the telephone, write notes, or send cards; it may be the ability to bring joy and hope as you visit in the home, hospital, or a nursing facility. Using any or all of these abilities will indicate that you and the church care about whatever is happening in these people's lives.

Most of all, be who you are. God does not call you to be perfect, just to be faithful and show that you care. If you take your position seriously, your life will never be the same. You will be blessed beyond anything you can imagine.

Develop listening ears. One symbol of friendship is the handshake. Another is the sharing of a hug. The symbol most needed in the church and world today, however, is the "cocked ear," the ability and willingness to listen. Listening is very difficult for many of us; we had rather talk. We need to develop that listening ear. When we really learn to listen, we will have something to say to those we serve.

As the spiritual leaders of the church, you will need to cultivate the habit of paying attention, not only to what is seen and heard, but also to what often goes unnoticed or unspoken. Learn to be observant and sense the need around you. Over the years I've suspected that individuals have come to worship and gone away with aching hearts, not because the members and elders did not care, but simply because they were too busy and failed to notice.

Develop that "cocked ear." Practice listening with your ears, and you will learn to love with your heart. Listen even to those who may seem dull and uninteresting. Listen to the children and those who wish they could become childlike again. They, too, have a story they want you to hear.

Practice the art of listening with your heart. Listening will be one of the most important things you do. During your tenure as an elder your heart is going to become populated with people. Howard Thurman once said that "ultimately there is only one place of refuge on the planet for any man and that is in another man's heart."[2] Your heart will feel very light and joyous as you share the high moments in people's lives, but it may feel heavy and overburdened as you share the pain and sorrow. It is important to remember that you do not serve alone; other elders and your pastor will be there to provide guidance and encouragement. God's presence will always be by your side. When your ears have been listening and your mind has been filled with concern, your heart will respond with whatever is right for that moment.

Develop the spirit of oneness as you serve at the Lord's table. Your presence and demeanor will be visible as you prepare the table and lead in prayer. This privilege will set you apart more than anything else you are called on to do. Communion unites those present in the sanctuary with those at home, those in the hospital, those in nursing and assisted living facilities, and even those on vacation. It binds us together as the body of Christ with him who is the head of the Church universal.

Many in the congregation will get to know you, your concern, compassion, and commitment, as they see you at the table. They will surely know if you are merely going through the motions. They will know as they see how the table has been prepared. They will know as they see you walk down the aisle. They will know as they watch you handle the bread and the cup and as they pray with you.

Elders always have been and always will be a powerful part of the system or symbols for the worshiper. One congregant was overheard commenting to another about an elder who had served at the table during a service that had just ended. "The witness of her life is so valuable to me! When she comes to lead me to communion, I see clearly the source of her kindness and am drawn by her to that source."

ADDRESS ELDERS

Each of you have been informed of the duties and responsibilities assigned to the office of elder. By your presence you have indicated your willingness to serve.

Do you believe that you have been called to eldership? Do you hear, feel, and accept Christ's call when he says, "Come, follow me." Do you accept that call? If so, will you respond by saying, "I will?"

ELDERS RESPOND:

I will.

ADDRESS THE CONGREGATION OR THOSE IN ATTENDANCE:

Each of you has indicated your willingness to support these persons as elders by electing them to the position and sharing with them in this installation. Do you accept these who stand before you as your spiritual leaders? Do you promise to support them by keeping them in your hearts and prayers. If so, please respond, "We will."

CONGREGATION RESPONDS:

We will.

THE PRESENTATION OF A SPECIAL GIFT

Minister or designated individual presents gift to each elder.

Closing prayer and benediction:

Go forth now from this place and walk in the power and presence of God, listening, sharing with, and serving those who need your guidance and presence in their lives. Through Christ's love we pray. Amen.

Service 2: Let Your Light Shine————————————

Leader

A pastor from Kansas shared this story in a church newsletter:

One dark and stormy night the power went off while I was in the midst of an elders' meeting. As always when we meet, a Christ candle burns, signifying the presence of the Holy Spirit in our midst. We already had "emergency lighting" in the room.

Amazed by the experience, I have pondered how significant the light of Christ becomes when other things are darkened. As I reflected on the moment, this spiritual came into my mind: "This little light of mine, I'm going to let it shine…let it shine, let it shine, all the time." Do you remember it? I have heard children singing it hundreds of times as they stood up on the chancel in front of the congregation. Nervously holding their little candles, watching the adult leader mouth the words, and becoming awestruck while staring at the small flame, one or two of them would unintentionally blow it out.

Then there were the red faces, in trouble because they had goofed up. I remember one little girl whose candle was only a smoking wick sang, "Make this little light of mine shine."

The little light glowed as it sat there on the coffee table in my office that dark night. We all stared at it while we talked of spiritual things and prayed. Before the lights went out, you could barely see the flame. I remember thinking that I needed to get a replacement candle so that the flame would be brighter. But when darkness fell upon the room, the little light began to fill the dark space with its soft calm light. A dim reflection fell on each elder and myself as we sat surrounding it. A gentle calmness seemed to settle within the depths of each person as the light of Christ shone on each one. We were taken by the holiness of its presence. On that dark and stormy night, a real Spirit moved in our midst. Even though it went unspoken, the presence of Christ was there.

Each time the elders gather, it is with the attitude of holiness. I always leave having been blessed. But that night, it was different. Oh, I know what you are thinking: a candle in a dark room is always comforting. Yes, it is. But not like it was that night.

As you begin your new term of service, a couple of things must be evident if the Spirit of God is to be strong in your presence.

First of all, you must be surrounded by a great cloud of witnesses. In other words, others must have the presence of Christ in them. "Therefore, since we are surrounded by so great a cloud of witnesses, let us also lay aside every weight, and sin which clings so closely, and let us run with perseverance the race that is set before us"(Heb. 12:1). When our elders met on that dark night, I had been extremely busy. It had been a draining week. But I was calmed and at peace in their presence.

Second, you must experience stillness. "Be still, and know that I am God" (Ps. 46:10a), the psalmist wrote. As I sat there in the presence of Christ's light, in the presence of the elders, for the first time that day and for most of the week, I was still. Then I realized that God is God. For me and you, that means everything.[3]

As you serve with your minister, let Christ's light shine upon you and within you. Then you will be surrounded by a great cloud of witnesses and will find the stillness and Spirit of God that will strengthen and guide you. When your light seems to go out, remember the little girl who sang, "Make this little light of mine shine."

By your presence here you acknowledge your acceptance and willingness to set aside time for study and prayer. You also acknowledge your willingness to serve and carry out the responsibilities of the office to which you have been chosen.

ADDRESS THE ELDERS:

If you accept these responsibilities, will you respond by saying, "I do, with God's spirit as my guide."

RESPONSE OF THE ELDERS:

I do, with God's spirit as my guide.

ADDRESS THE CONGREGATION OR OTHERS IN ATTENDANCE:

If you, as members of the congregation, accept these who have been chosen to be your spiritual leaders, will you promise to support them by sharing the light of God's presence? If so, please respond by saying, "I will let the light of Christ shine though me."

RESPONSE OF CONGREGATION OR OTHERS PRESENT:

I will let the light of Christ shine through me.

PRESENTATION OF SPECIAL GIFT

(Minister or designated individual presents each elder with a gift.)

BENEDICTION:

Spirit of the living God, fall afresh on those who have been chosen to lead this congregation. Strengthen, guide, and enfold them with your love as they go forth to serve in your name. Amen.

Maundy Thursday Dinner and Lord's Supper

Service 1: In Remembrance of Me————————————————

PARTICIPANTS

Minister (or chosen leader), elders, deacons, pianist, choir or other special music, and committee to plan and coordinate the meal preparation and serving of the meal.

INVITATIONS

One of the best and most intimate ways to show our friends we care is to invite them to dinner. Christ invited his friends to dinner one night many years ago. He shared his thoughts and feelings, but more importantly he shared his love. What better way to share in the celebration of the Lord's supper than to invite your church family to dinner. There you may share concern and love for one another as you receive the continuing love of Jesus Christ.

Enclose the invitation in the church bulletin or newsletter, and mail to shut-ins and inactive members. Prepare fliers and post in classrooms and on bulletin boards.

SUGGESTED WORDING FOR INVITATION
Front cover of folded invitation:

"HOLY THURSDAY"

(purple or lavender paper *with picture of bread and chalice*)

Inside cover:

"The Worship Department—
Minister, Elders, and Deacons of
(*YOUR TOWN*) CHRISTIAN CHURCH
request the honor of your presence
for dinner, fellowship and celebration of
THE LORD'S SUPPER
on Thursday evening—(*date*)
from–(*hours*).

Please bring a dish to share. Meat, beverages, and bread will be provided.

Kindly make a reservation by marking your Sunday attendance slip or by calling the church office

(*telephone number*) by (*date*)."

Materials needed

Speaker's stand or lectern, invitations, bulletins, hymnals (or include words in bulletin), tablecloths, candles, pillar candle, candle lighters, communion service, bread, juice, large loaf of bread, fresh grapes, food for meal as promised in invitation.

Setting

Arrange the tables in the shape of a cross. This is done by placing a large round table in the center of the room and placing rectangular tables in four directions to form the cross. The length and width will depend on the number of attendees expected. If a round table is not available, check with a department store. Many use them for displays and may be willing to loan one to the church.

Cover the tables using either cloth or paper.

Build a column in center of the round table using cheese boxes, hat boxes, or anything round that is available. Drape with a purple cloth. Form a centerpiece on top using the loaf of bread, grapes, and the pillar candle.

Place four (or number needed) communion trays at the locations where the tables meet. Reserve eight chairs (or number needed) for the deacons at locations nearest the trays. It is from this point that the deacons will pick up the trays and serve those seated at their tables.

Place votive candles (in holders) at intervals down the center of the tables. You may also use battery-operated votive candles available from craft stores, or strings of the tiny battery-operated lights. Ivy or other greens can be used to cover the wires.

Place other candles at appropriate locations around the room: on top of the piano and in windows if you have them. Be sure to put all candles in holders for protection against fire.

At the appropriate time, the deacons, youth, or other designated individuals will light the candles. If battery-operated candles or lights are used, they will flip the switch to turn these on, or individuals seated near those candles may be asked to perform this task.

After dinner, when the candles have been lit and the other lights have been dimmed or turned off, the form of the cross will be seen. This is an inspiring scene for observing the Lord's supper or closing the service, whichever you choose.

SUGGESTED HYMNS

" Here at Thy Table, Lord," *Chalice Hymnal,* no. 384

"According to Thy Gracious Word, " *Chalice Hymnal,* no. 402

"In Remembrance of Me," *Chalice Hymnal,* no. 403

"Break Thou the Bread of Life," *Chalice Hymnal,* no. 321

BULLETIN OUTLINE

Blessing for Meal
Dinner
Gathering Music—choir, solo, or instrumental
Opening Hymn
Meditation
Hymn of Communion
Words of Institution
Prayers for the Bread and Cup
Sharing of the Bread and Cup
Friendship Circle
Benediction
Closing Hymn: "Blest Be the Tie That Binds"

GATHERING MUSIC

(Choir anthem, solo, or quiet music while participants take their places at various spots around the table and acolytes or designated persons light the candles located around the room and on the table.

OPENING HYMN

MEDITATION

There is no time more fitting for observing the Lord's supper than on this evening, the evening of a day set aside as Maundy Thursday. Jesus had spent the day in retirement at Bethany…He knew full well what the night and the next day would bring him.

Again and again we are told that he saw what was awaiting him in that city. He was ready for the scourging, the mockery, the crown of thorns, the hours of agony, and the darkness of his death. During those long days of teaching, healing, and unselfish service he saw clearly the outline of the cross.

He was concerned, but the Bible indicates that his thoughts continually turned toward the disciples and the message he would bring them at the evening meal. He knew what it would mean to them and to him. As he sat at the table, he declared something of the burden he had been carrying for them during the day:

> And he said to them, "I have earnestly desired to eat this passover with you before I suffer; for I tell you I shall not eat it until it is fulfilled in the kingdom of God." (Lk. 22:15–16)

Tonight we are seated at the cross to remind us of what tomorrow will bring. We come as did the early disciples to share a meal with him. Let us prepare our hearts to receive him.

HYMN OF COMMUNION
"In Remembrance of Me," *Chalice Hymnal,* no. 403 or
"Break Thou the Bread of Life," *Chalice Hymnal,* no. 321

WORDS OF INSTITUTION—MINISTER

OBSERVANCE OF LORD'S SUPPER
Prayers for the Bread and Cup—*Elders*
Sharing of the Bread and Cup—*Deacons*

FRIENDSHIP CIRCLE
Formed at the direction of the minister or leader, who asks guests to stand, join hands, and form a circle around the tables. This is very effective as the lights on the table form a cross.

BENEDICTION–MINISTER:
Having communed with you, O Lord, and with each other in this special place and with hearts made warm and wills made strong again through the receiving of the bread and cup, we now return to our homes. Continue to surround us with your presence that we may stand with you as you face the cross. Amen.

CLOSING HYMN:
"Blest Be the Tie That Binds," *Chalice Hymnal,* no. 433

Service 2: Come Break the Bread————————————

SUGGESTED PROGRAM OUTLINE
- Gathering time, welcoming, and grace for the meal
- Meal served with discussions taking place at each table
- Brief break as tables are cleared and participants take their places
- Special Music—choir, solo, or instrumental
- Meditation—"Come Break the Bread"—presented by minister or designated person
- Hymn of Communion: "Come, Share the Lord," verses 1 and 2, *Chalice Hymnal,* no. 408
- Words of Institution—minister
- Prayers for the Bread and the Cup—designated elders
- Sharing of the Bread and the Cup at each table

- Closing Hymn:
  "We Call Ourselves Disciples," verses 1 and 5, *Chalice Hymnal,* no. 357
- Benediction—minister

PARTICIPANTS

The minister or other designated leader to preside and give the communion meditation and words of institution, plus two elders to offer the prayer for the Bread and the Cup. These persons may be seated at the same table or at three different tables and stand and share at the appropriate time.

Two individuals to lead at each table: one person to serve as host or hostess and lead the discussion, and an elder to preside over the Lord's supper. The number of persons needed will depend on the number of tables.

A committee to decide on the type of meal that will be served—covered dish or one prepared by a class or department—and to oversee the set-up, preparation, serving, and clean-up after the service.

SETTING

Separate tables arranged to each seat twelve people if possible.

TABLE ARRANGEMENTS

Breads representing different countries, pitchers of juice, chalices, and printed sheets of information to be used as discussion starters. Place a loaf of partially cut bread on each table along with a pitcher of juice and a chalice or glass. Use a small card to identify the bread and the country it represents.

A listing of breads that individuals can make or may be purchased from a bakery or grocery, and the country they represent, follows:

Austria—Sourdough Rye Bread
Belize—Coconut Bread
Ethiopia—Spicy Tea Bread

Germany—Hearty Wheat Bread
Ireland—Raisin Bread
Jamaica—Banana Bread
United States—Kentucky Corn Bread
West Bank (Middle East)—Pita Bread

DISCUSSION STARTERS

Make copies of the following information and place copies on each table as guides for discussion during the dinner. As you share the meal together, discuss the significance of bread.

"To the person who has but one meal a day, the only form in which God dare appear is bread."—GANDHI

Bread for myself is a material concern; bread for others is a spiritual concern.

"Bread is one of the most simple, basic foods we know, yet it offers a wealth of images. In the Judeo-Christian tradition, bread is a symbol of such widely contrasting concepts as suffering, hope, liberation, and reconciliation. Before the captive Israelites made their exodus from Egypt, they prepared an unleavened 'bread of affliction' (Deut. 16:3). It symbolized the suffering of their soon-to-end slavery and the difficult road they would walk to freedom.

During the Israelites' forty-year wilderness pilgrimage, God provided manna, a bread that liberated them from desert hunger. Many years later, when Jesus multiplied a few barley loaves to feed a crowd of Jewish people living under Roman occupation, the people connected this bread with the manna their ancestors ate and longed for their own liberation.

Jesus ate bread with friends and multiplied it for the poor. He described his kingdom as yeast that penetrated and expanded the gluten of grain. But, most importantly, he took for himself the identity of bread. In order to bring reconciliation between peoples, and between people and God, he allowed others to break his body and take his life."[4]

MEDITATION

Minister or designated person:

So they drew near to the village to which they were going. He appeared to be going further, but they constrained him, saying, "Stay with us, for it is toward evening and the day is now far spent." So he went in to stay with them. When he was at table with them, he took the bread and blessed, and broke it, and gave it to them. And their eyes were opened and they recognized him; and he vanished out of their sight. (Lk. 24:28–31)

During the walk to Emmaus, the two disciples did not recognize Jesus. Not until he blessed the bread and broke it did they remember him. "Their eyes were opened and they recognized him." Halford E. Luccock says that they knew him only when they remembered the familiar motions when he broke the bread.[5] So it is with us tonight. We sometimes do not recognize or even remember him until we come about his table. We recognize him as we share bread with others, in the way we break bread and divide it. Dr. Luccock, through his writings, teaches us that even today Christ is made known to men and women who see us break and share bread. In our unselfish dealing with our bread, they see the Christ who said, "It is more blessed to give than to receive" (Acts 20:35).

Let us remember that Christ will be made known to those who do not know him, not only by what we say, but by the qualities of Christ made evident as we live from day to day. Let us prepare our hearts to receive him: "Come, take the bread, come, drink the wine, come, share the Lord."

HYMN OF COMMUNION

"Come, Share the Lord," verses 1 and 2, *Chalice Hymnal,* no. 408.

COMMUNION

Following the singing of the communion hymn, the minister and the selected elders will give the invitation to communion and prayers. The presiding elder at each table will serve the bread and the cup to the person seated to the left and on around the table until the elder has been served and returns the bread and the cup to the table.

CLOSING HYMN

"We Call Ourselves Disciples," verses 1 and 5, *Chalice Hymnal,* no. 357

BENEDICTION

Go now from these tables, where we have been separate but one, remembering that the presence of Jesus Christ will be with you as often as you invite him to come share the bread. Amen.

Alternative Worship Service[6]
The Open Table: Food for Life

The minister and the board of elders at East Aurora, Christian Church, in East Aurora, New York, began discussions concerning the possibility of starting an alternative worship service. Two criteria became priorities. The service would be held on a weeknight and would follow Disciples tradition and begin with a meal. Two other things were also central. There would be Bible study and discussion followed by the celebration of the Lord's supper. Those in attendance include those who regularly attend Sunday morning worship as well as those whose work schedule prohibits them from worshiping during the morning hour or on the weekend. The first service was held in December 2004 and has continued each Thursday evening at 6:30 p.m.

Suggestions for Setting Up This Service

Arrange the tables in a rectangular configuration so those in attendance can face each other. When the group is small, two rectangular tables are used; but others can be added as needed. Small loaves of bread and small pitchers of juice with individual plastic cups are placed on each table.

Volunteers are secured the week before each service to provide a part of the meal, such as soup and/or sandwiches, salad, bread, and a desert.

The minister, several elders, or other volunteers accept the responsibility for the discussion around a particular theme chosen the week before. Those leaders prepare worship folders, which are placed on a table for individuals to pick up as they arrive. The folders contain quotes, scriptures, and questions for consideration on the chosen theme.

The themes often depend on the season of the year and current local or national issues. They vary from baptism, communion, the trinity, or the message from the cross to the needs of the community and the root causes of hunger. For the summer months a series such as "Who Is Jesus?" is chosen.

At 6:30 p.m. the group gathers.

A time of sharing takes place as individuals arrive and catch up on what's happening in each other's lives and the life of the congregation.

At 6:40 the meal and community time begins.

Following the meal, the discussion, often led by the minister, begins. It concludes with prayer and communion. The prayers for the loaf and the cup are offered by the elders. The bread is passed around the table, with each individual breaking off a piece. Then the pitcher is passed, with each person pouring the juice for the person seated next to him or her. The emblems are held, and all partake simultaneously. Or, the bread and the pitcher may be passed with each individual partaking at own discretion.

The praying of the Lord's Prayer together concludes the service.

Baptismal Meditation

Baptism Offers Newness of Life

Jesus undoubtedly lived a simple life in the little village of Nazareth. He would surely have helped his mother about the house and his father in his carpenter's shop. We know that as he grew older he was thinking deeply and striving to discover what the will of God was for him.

Some years passed, and Jesus, as a young man, joined with others to go to the valley of the Jordan. The Jordan is a unique river that springs from four main sources and eventually pours some six million cubic meters of water per day into the Dead Sea. Jesus journeyed to this river to see and hear John the Baptist. John was preaching the coming of the kingdom of God on earth; and Jesus, wanting to be a part of the newly forming kingdom community, requested that John baptize him.

Scripture tells us that: "In those days Jesus came from Nazareth of Galilee and was baptized by John in the Jordan. And when he came up out of the water, immediately he saw the heavens opened and the Spirit descending upon him like a dove; and a voice came from heaven, 'Thou art my beloved Son; with thee I am well pleased'" (Mk. 1:9–11).

After his baptism, he went into the wilderness and stayed for forty days and nights in meditation and prayer. The late Colbert S. Cartwright affirms that baptism is the first step on our lifetime journey of growth and commitment. It is a time of "inner spiritual renewal." It is both a personal and a social action in which an individual undertakes a new life of Christian discipleship within the fellowship of the whole people of God—Christ's church.[7]

Those who come to be baptized this day no doubt have traveled a journey similar to the one Jesus traveled. To be sure, you may not have lived in the same little village, grown up in the same type of house, or performed the same kind of chores; but you have been on your own spiritual journey. You come now, not to the Jordan, but to this place to be among your friends who welcome you as a part of the fellowship that gathers here for worship. You have come to continue your spiritual journey of prayer and service.

The Preamble to the Disciples Design of the Christian Church states: "Through baptism into Christ we enter into newness of life and are made one with the whole people of God."

Come now and begin your journey of newness of life with Christ Jesus and your family of faith.[8]

Praying for Those Who Are Sick

Arthur H. Becker suggests, "It is important that we develop the facility for speaking to God on behalf of others, in the simple language of a child making a request of a beloved father."[9]

As we visit with individuals who are hospitalized, in rehabilitation, in nursing facilities, or recovering in their homes, the important thing to do is listen.

Learn to listen carefully to what is said and not said during those moments preceding the prayer time. This will provide clues as to what needs to be included in our prayer on their behalf. Mr. Becker advises that, "Prayer is not a lecture to the person we are visiting; it is our collection of that person's expressed concerns brought before God."[10]

Prayer Lines

The following are provided as seed thoughts for your prayers.

Great Physician, place your loving arms around (*patient's name*) that the warm embrace of your healing love may be felt.

Strengthen (*name*) that she may overcome the doubt and anxiety that is so much a part of her feelings at this time. Give her courage and renewed faith in Jesus Christ, the Great Physician, as she faces surgery (*or* tests).

Loving Father, the source of our hope and strength, be with and bless (*name*), who must spend this night in the hospital (*or* rehabilitation center or nursing facility.) (*Name*), may your faith in the Great Physician strengthen you with a night's rest and bring strength for what lies ahead.

Most gracious and loving heavenly Father, as you travel the corridors of this facility, bring your tender mercy to (*name*) and all others who need your healing. Guide the hearts, minds, and hands of the medical personnel, the specialists, and the technicians that they may receive strength from you as they care for others.

Prayers for Those Who Are Grieving

The most shattering experience that can befall the human spirit is the death of a loved one. The loss affects the head, heart, and spirit. There are so many decisions and choices to be made, so many tasks to complete, so many people to greet, so many tears that won't stop flowing, so many questions for which there are no immediate answers. Sometime in those periods of feeling all alone, meditative prayers may bring comfort. The prayers that follow are basically for use by persons who are grieving. The thoughts they contain, however, may be helpful to those who are trying to understand the pain and hurt they are experiencing.

O Lord, you know that I have many private fears. I am afraid to share them with others, lest they perceive me as being weak. Some days I want to be left alone, and on other days I fear having to someday live alone. On other days I feel alone even when in a crowd. Sometimes I fear that when my initial grief and hurt has eased, my family and friends will be too busy living their own lives to spend time with me. Let painful memories of the past fade away that I may face tomorrow unafraid. Amen.

O Lord, right now there is so much pain in my life. Please quiet my trembling heart long enough for me to recognize and be grateful for the joys of the past, for my family and friends, for the laughter and excitement of children, for the fellowship shared with my neighbors and community. Guide and sustain me that I may touch and love, laugh and cry, and give hope to myself and to others. Amen.

O Lord, I remember how you touched those who were sick, lonely, and in need of a friend. Help me to be receptive to the patience and caring of family and friends as they share in my grief. May I yield to their love and to you, allowing you even now to mold me and make me into what I can become as I face an uncertain future. Amen.

Communion Resources

Meditation 1 — We Come as Disciples—————————————

We come to your table from many addresses, responding to your request that we "do this in remembrance of you." We come to your table that stands front and center not only here in this sanctuary but front and center in the member churches of the Christian Church (Disciples of Christ).

We come knowing that we are all welcome at this table because our founding father, young Alexander Campbell, believed so strongly in Christian unity and the openness of the Lord's supper that he boldly approached the table in the 1840s, placed his admission token on the table, and declared that since you are the host, who are we to keep anyone away?

We come as a family made up of individuals of all ages, economic backgrounds, and racial and ethnic backgrounds. We come each with our own personality and our own needs. We come knowing that you will accept us just as we are.

We come now to be fed as we partake of this bread that represents your broken body and the fruit of the vine that represents your blood shed. As we prepare to receive this small piece of bread and the juice from this tiny cup, we feel your presence with us. May we be strengthened and empowered to go forth from this place both willing and able to listen with our hearts as we witness and practice our faith in a broken world.

Meditation 2—The Lord Prepares a Table————————

As we gather around this table with fellow Christians, the communities from which we come are in relative peace and calm. No guns were aimed, and no bombs were thrown. No words of hatred were shouted as we passed by. Yet as we worship, we know that delegations are gathering around other tables in many parts of your broken world; negotiations are being made to ward off war and hostility or to negotiate a peace where there is already conflict.

We come before you because we want to find comfort and peace in this place with you around your table. As we come, the psalmist continues to remind us: "The Lord prepares a table before us in the presence of our enemies" (Ps. 23:5a, paraphrase). History confirms that the table has always been set in the presence of enemies; even the upper room held a betrayer.

We are thankful that we belong to a church community that always has "a table before us" as a reminder of the Christ who came to serve and teach us how to love even our enemies. As we receive the bread and the cup representing your broken body and shed blood, continue to remind us that others need to be invited to this table of forgiveness and grace.

The table is ready. Come meet Christ here.

Meditation 3—Lord, Make Us One————————

On Sunday morning as we filed into the ballroom for worship, we stopped at the entrance to be counted. The assistant to the priest took a wafer and placed it in a special container for each person as we entered. I turned to my host and said: "I don't think I am supposed to commune." She replied, " You have been the guest speaker for our assembly. If the bishop denies you communion, I will not partake either." At the appropriate time we filed forward. When I reached the bishop—I knew him well—he looked at me. My host nodded to him, and I was served. The next time I saw the bishop neither of us mentioned the service.

Some years later, Dr. Clark and I were traveling in South Africa for Church Women United. One Sunday, prior to worship, we shared breakfast with a Anglican priest and his family. So far no mention had been made regarding our denominational affiliation. however, the priest knew from the biographical data he had received.

We were welcomed at the beginning of the service. Then he stated that special permission had been received from the bishop for me to participate in holy communion. Since Dr. Clark was a member of the American Episcopal Church, no permission was required for her. In both instances, I was permitted to come to the table. I felt very close to Alexander Campbell as I did. I wasn't required to have a token, but I felt as if I needed one.

Disciples are very strong on Christian unity. Someone has pointed out that the very word *communion* has "union" in it. Here we are one because we are his. We come at his invitation. His sacrifice brings us together at the table.

Holy communion bids us to look beyond the confines of the sanctuary to a world torn by starvation, hatred, and war. Christ came to save others just as truly as he came to seek and save those of us who happen to have been born in a more favored place. Here at his table, we are one with the cathedral and the thatched chapel. We are one with the Gothic church and the storefront meeting houses.

As we partake of the emblems, we become one with his followers around the world. Some will be kneeling at altars, some will be seated, and others will be standing. Many will receive the wafer from the hand of the priest, while others will take the emblems themselves. The words spoken will vary, but inherent in them will be the phrase, "Do this in remembrance of me." Lord, make us one!

Communion Prayers————————————

We gather at your table, O Lord, as a part of your worldwide family who has been coming about the table since day began to break on the Tongo Islands. We are reminded as we come that this table extends around the world, and that long after we have departed from this place others will still be gathering in churches, both large and small, in tents and open fields, in secret places and on the battlefield to give thanks for the sacrifice you made for each of us.

We come confessing that we have spoken when we should have been silent; we have been silent when we should have spoken. We have committed sins of omission and commission since we last gathered here.

As we partake of the bread and the cup, help us to remember that forgiveness, cleansing, healing, and renewal can come into each of our lives if we would but submit them unto you. Renew a spirit of family within us when we leave this place, and guide us that we may carry the message of your love to all we meet. We pray in the name of Jesus Christ our Savior and the Prince of Peace. Amen.

PRAYER FOR THE BREAD

O God, you who are so like a forgiving father and a nurturing mother, we come to you on this day of Jesus' command, seeking to know how to "love one another." Help us to see, O God of life, that it is in receiving your love for us that we will be able to love one another. We approach this table with trembling hearts because we are so deeply touched by your love for us as we experience it in Jesus. Jesus loved us enough, not only to wash our feet, but to die for us. As we partake of the bread, O God, be in us with love, a love that will turn us upside down: from self-centered to other-centered, from narrow to open, from down to up, from despairing to hope filled. Thank you, O God, for your love that gives us new life. This we pray in Jesus' loving name. Amen.[11]

CHRIS HOBGOOD

PRAYER FOR THE CUP

Eternal God, whose will took Jesus to the cross, help us know that to follow you is to go all the way with you. Forgive us when we take lightly your mandate to love one another. Remind us again that Jesus didn't just say this, he did it. Help us to know that you are demanding of us, for you ask our all. Yet you are also the one who first loved us. You never ask of us more than you have already given. Now give us, with this cup, the power to go forth and live your love in every way. In the name of Jesus who gave his life for each one of us. Amen.[12]

CHRIS HOBGOOD

Poems————————————————————————

"As Long as Mankind Prays"

The Master shared plain bread with those who loved
   Him
On that night before the fatal plot was laid.
The blessing that He spoke made all the bread sacred;
As long as mankind prays—
   "Give us this day our daily bread."

Within the cup His holy face reflected
Bore lines of anguish for His undiscerning friends,
But loyal love shone from His eyes to pardon their
   stumbling minds—
As long as mankind prays—
   "Forgive us our transgressions."

For living bread our hungry souls are yearning;
Our thirsty spirits crave that cup divine.
No barriers of race or creed or nation
Can break that sacramental comradeship of bread and
   wine
As long as mankind prays —
   "Our Father Who Art in Heaven."

DR. PERRY E. GRESHAM [13]

Notes

Meditations for the Church Year

[1]Dorothy D. France, *Partners in Prayer* (St. Louis, Mo.: CBP Press, 1986), adapted.

[2]Thomas á Kempis, *The Imitation of Christ*, book 2, chapter 3.

[3]Phillips Brooks, "O Little Town of Bethlehem," written in 1868, verse 4, *Chalice Hymnal* (St. Louis: Chalice Press, 1995), no. 144.

[4]Mimi Weaver, "Building Bridges," *Update*, a newsletter of Richmond Hill in Richmond, Virginia, Expanding the Circle column.

[5]Widely quoted online, sometimes attributed to no one, sometimes to Toyohiko Kagawa, a Japanese author and activist.

[6]Robert A. F. Thurman, *Anger*, The Seven Deadly Sins (New York: New York Public Library, Oxford Univ. Press, 2005).

[7]Henri J. M. Nouwen, *Making All Things New: An Invitation to the Spiritual Life* (San Francisco: Harper & Row, 1981), 69–70.

[8]George Herbert, "Let All the World in Every Corner Sing," verse 2, in *Hymnbook for Christian Worship* (St. Louis, Mo.: Bethany Press, 1970), 83.

[9]Lin D. Cartwright, "Drawn Out of Darkness," *The Christian* (April 5, 1964): 2.

[10]Dorothy D. France with Jason and David Frankle, *You Might Be A Football Fan if…*(Berea, Ohio: Quixote Publications, 2000). Available from ddfenprise@aol.com.

[11]James S. Stewart, *The Wind of the Spirit* (Nashville: Abingdon Press, 1968), 10, 11.

[12]Maude Mayes, Petersburg, Virginia. Included in a personal gift to me of a collection of her prayers received before her death.

[13]Rosa Page Welch, "The Miracle of Communion," *Chalice Hymnal* (St. Louis: Chalice Press, 1995), no. 412.

[14]Thomas Cotterill, "In Memory of the Savior's Love," words written in 1805, *Chalice Hymnal* (St. Louis: Chalice Press, 1995), no. 405.

[15]Dwight E. Stevenson, *Your Face in This Mirror* (St. Louis: Bethany Press, 1959), 42–43.

[16]Dwight E. Stevenson, "Discover the Book of Luke for Yourself," in *The Bethany Church School Guide* (December 1948): 108.

Meditations for the Civil Year

[1]O. I. Cricket Harrison, "Restless Weaver," words written in 1988 and revised in 1993, *Chalice Hymnal* (St. Louis: Chalice Press, 1995), no. 658.

[2]From "Freedom Isn't Free," © Up With People, Inc.

[3]Charles Kingsley, *The Water Babies* (New York: F.A. Stokes, 1891).

[4]Henry Wadsworth Longfellow, "A Psalm of Life," available online through www.poetryfoundation.org.

[5]From the Wikipedia Web site descriptions of the history of Thanksgiving in the United States and Canada, www.wikipedia.org.

Meditations for Days In-Between

[1]Some sources cite author unknown, but others give Myra Goodwin Plantz (1856–1914) as the poet who penned these lines.

Special Services

[1]Sebastian Temple, "Take My Hands," © 1967 OCP Publications, 5536 N.E. Hassalo, Portland, OR 97213.

[2]Howard Thurman , *Strange Freedom* (Boston: Beacon Press, 1998).

[3]Adapted for this installation service from a column by the Rev. John Albert Gran, First Christian Church, McPherson, Kansas. Used with his permission.

[4]Joetta Handrich Schlabach, *Extending the Table* (Scottdale, Pa.: Herald Press, 1991), 45.

[5]Halford E. Luccock, *Never Forget to Live* (Nashville: Abingdon Press, 1961).

[6]The suggestion and guidance for this service were provided by the Rev. Amos Acree, minister of East Aurora Christian Church (Disciples of Christ) located in East Aurora, New York.

[7]Colbert S. Cartwright, *People of the Chalice* (St. Louis: Chalice Press, 1988).

[8]Small bottles of water from the Jordan River may be purchased from Christian Book Stores and used as a part of this service. The minister lifts up the bottle of water and states, for example, "Jesus was baptized in the Jordan. I now pour water from the Jordan River into your baptismal waters."

[9]Arthur H. Becker, *The Compassionate Visitor* (Minneapolis: Augsburg,1985), 75.

[10]Ibid., 77.

[11]W. Chris Hobgood, "He Loved Them to the End," in *At Christ's Table,* ed. Dorothy D. France (St. Louis: Chalice Press, 1997), 62.

[12]Ibid.

[13]Dr. Perry E. Gresham, "As Long as Mankind Prays," quoted in *Special Days of the Church Year* (St. Louis, Mo.: Bethany Press, 1969), 218.